SCANDALOUS VENDETTA

The temperature is at its highest ninety eight degrees to be exact. Remarkably lovely! The environments at peace for once this week. The sky-scrapers in the city are producing lots of shade and people are enjoying the great weather. It's the first day of summer and the sun's ultra rays are beaming, beautiful women in short-shorts, turning heads as they walk by with their hour-glassed shaped figures. There stood this one women in front of the local supermarket," boy oh boy" ,I deceive you not, wearing an all baby blue summer sleeveless skirt with sandals to match and standing out like a hot diamond. Her name MISS MARTHA JEFFRIES

Her measurements 35-24-37,Height5"9.Golden brown complexion, gorgeous hazel eyes ,longjet black hair that ended at the curve of her lower back. Martha's from the beautiful island of Jamaica, with a compelling blend of Asian, twenty-five years old and127 pounds of pure beauty, at its best .Her family migrated to Central America four and a half decades ago after world war two. Growing up under the custody of her granny, her and her younger brother Danny. A terrible plane crash which took the lives of their parents and Grandfather, every winter she would visit her only ANNE MAE, who owned a large clothing store in Kingston,Jamaica.

Standing outside the market alone waiting for her granny, she thinks to herself "GOD IT's HOT"! And as the sun is gleaming off her beautiful body she's moist with sweat. She looks thru her matching baby blue purse searching for a cloth and her sunglasses, she finds them both and wipes her forehead slowly........cars blowing their horns as she slowly walks towards the bus stop and takes a seat. A burgundy jeep wrangler pulls alongside her," Good Lord! Look what we have here." The passenger said. OH! Excuse my rudeness young lady." As he desperately undressed her. " Today must be your birthday and I was wondering, if I can have a piece of your cake?" Giving his homeboy a high five. "You scored my nig, you scored!" " I sure did son! HA-HA!" Not paying them any mind and being taught the facts of life by her grandmother instilled morals and respect in oneself. However, ignoring them would bring problems and hating men who paid more attention to her body than her personality made her extremely emotional. Looking in another direction before slowly crossing her legs. The man who spoke to her was looking directly up her skirt. The driver in the jeep said in a sarcastic manner. "Why are you acting like it's all about you!" Saying to herself, "If he only knew, it's all about me."

At this time another vehicle pulls up, a 1998 190 SLK convertible 2 door green Mercedes Benz. The driver of the jeep acknowledges the car's presence. "Who's that behind us?! " " It's ,that crazy ass Jamaican boy Danny......AH Shit Man!" "WHAT!" "He's getting out with his right hand in his waist!" "Just be cool we have a treaty remember?" Danny approaches the jeep slow-stepping, and in a forceful low-tone he said, "Aren't we out of our jurisdiction boys? You know the rules, and I know none of you blood clots trying to hit on my sister." The driver said. " OH no, no one's doing that!" "You know it's been kind of quiet lately no funerals!... I know yall would like to keep it like that?" "No question!... In fact, we didn't even know that was your sister." Martha starts thinking to herself, should I tell him the truth, no I better not cause he just came home from jail and plus I want him home with mother and I. We need him out here not in there and I hate visiting him in prison. The passenger spoke out respectfully, "We were just leaving man." Danny giving them this evil look before saying, "WHAT'S THE HOLD UP!" Immediately peeling off leaving massive smoke. Danny drew his 45 automatic and aimed it directly at their gas tank. "No Danny!" Martha yells, "Are you going crazy or did you just lose your mind?"   "FUCK THEM!!!!!!" he barked.   "You're absolutely right however, your freedom comes first and, I'm not about to run back and forth to prison every week, If you catch another bid, do you hear me? "Yeah, Yeah, Yeah."   "You don't own no areas around here, the white man does and he's going to lock you up the minute you start claiming them....Didn't you learn your lesson yet? How many friends you've lost?"   "Too many."   "You need to get out of America for a while, why don't you visit home. I know uncle Jamel would love to see you and it's been about, what? 7 years, and he's your favorite uncle."   Mumbling to himself, "He's our only uncle." Poor Danny he was already labeled as the rude boy of the ghettos and a notorious drug dealer. However he was smart enough to open up a legitimate business in his grandmother's name. "Girl what are you doing sitting at the bus station all alone looking hot? He asked.   "Boy please I'm waiting on mama" she responded dryly. " How could you be waiting on mama and she's in the house chilling under the air conditioner."   "Oh, you went to get her?"   "Yes I did, and I told you once before if you need a ride anywhere take one of my cabs."   "Damn I feel so embarrassed."   "I would too, sitting in this hot ass sun sweating like a foul pig." They started laughing and she was sweating like crazy. However, Danny does the honors and opens the car door for his stunning sister.   "Why thank you lil brah."   "You're welcome big sis."   "Don't drive me straight home I want to ride around with you for a while, and catch some of this cool breeze, if you don't mind."   "You joking sis."   "No I'm not, let's go." Squealing off while making a u turn, and the light changes right on time. They were very close he would die and kill for her and vice versa on her part. Danny took care of the family, however Martha wants her own and unfortunately opportunities are not knocking at her door. Four years of college in America seems like a waste and faithfully dedicating all of her time to her school work. Majoring in four courses, day and night classes, summer school as well. Marketing telecommunications, computer technician and MBA in accounting. Doing her brothers books for his business, helped to keep him out of federal prison. Handling all the bills, taxes, payroll, and his high cost of living, something for her to do, but not enough.

chapter 2

"Girl let's go hang out tonight!" Tiffany said, "Where?" Martha asked,"I don't know......"Let's just go walking and catch some cool night breeze." "Tiffany girl you know I don't play the streets." "Girl you need to start dating and come out the house." "I don't know girl."   " What are you afraid of?" "Your damn brother's home now and i must say UHM,UHM,UHM,! it was worth the wait!" "You slept with him already?" "Now girl you know he had to taste some of his native heritage before he smelt one of those American women.You see gal if he wants his dick sucked he goes to one of them,on the other hand if he wants some goood or should I say great punanny mixed with loving, he knows how to find me."   They laugh.   "What's so funny girls?" grandmother asked. "Nothing!" "I wanna laugh too darling." Her grandmother had this very ancestral accent a full blooded Jamaican with pure passion and deep love for others. "Girl stop making me laugh because grandma is being nosey over here."   still she was giggling and grandma was being even nosier. "listen i'mma stop making you laugh but you must promise me you're going to hang out with me and Yasha tonight." "Girl ,I'll just hang up on you if I wanna stop laughing." " I bet you would too and I'll pound you out when I see you tomorrow." "Tiffany, you know you ain't built like that, so don't play yourself or you're going to find yourself by yourself." "You know I love you girl and i would never hurt you." "me too baby." "So that means you're hanging out with us tonight?" "Yes it does." "I can't believe it!" "Calm down girl!"...."What should I wear?" "Something tight and freaky" "Get out of here!..I'mma wear some baggy jeans and a sweatshirt" "Girl let them see something!" "Hell No! If a man chooses me it will be because of my personality,not my body or looks." "You should'nt do that to yourself Martha." "What do you mean?" " Show that beautiful body of yours,with those beautiful bust sitting at attention and that bodacious ass turning heads everytime you step out the house." "Girl are you crazy? Ain't my brother enough for you, and john-john?" "Don't be watching me!" " I know you ain't getting like these american girls are we?" "Please,john-john is my good guy and your brother is my bad guy....You know damn well i'm strickly dickly and just to let you know i judge everything okay!" "Well excuse me for inquiring." "That's right don't be an inquiring mind cause girlfriend ,you really don't want to know!" much laughter. "Can I laugh with y'all?" "Is that grandma again?" "YES child,let me get off this phone and get ready." "Tell grandma I love her." "Okay I'll see you soon,bye!" "Bye!" "Grandma, Tiffany said she loves you!" "I love her too!" Walking towards her room,contemplating on what to wear, something tight, to come to think of it,I don't have anything tight. She has a strong native accent also.

One hour later 9:00p.m. Martha comes out of her room looking like a tom-boy,with her chicago bulls sweatsuit,matching hat and the star players jersey.We all know who that is, along with the footwear, female Air Jordans. She had small feet a size 6 and a half and her behind still was noticable. Looking at herself in the mirror and shaking her head in a horizontal motion. Trying her best to hide her breast and buttocks. "DAMN!" she whispers. "Nothing won't work!" Grandma creeps behind her before saying. "You can't hide that babydoll." "OHH grandma you startled me." "I'm so sorry sweety,but look at mines." Lord have mercy, she had a big rump on her and a nice set of breast,38D-30-40-,and look good for her age 62,height 5'8 and a half,weight 169 pounds. "Yo grandfather loved rubbing up on this ting.You go out there and have a good time,don't hide it flaunt it.....You still a virgin aren't you?" "Yes grandma." Before placing her palms on martha's face and kissing her,she said"Remember these words, respect and trust goes along way.If he possesses those qualities,then he's worthy of those jewels you were blessed with by GOD." "What are those jewels?"martha asked. "Your heart,which is procreated by your womb." "and how will i know if he's the right one grandma?"As a tiny sparkle of water falls from beneath her eyes. "Baby I can't answer dat,however,you and only you will know." "Thank you grandma and i love you so much!"giving her a big hug. "Stop shedding those tears,no baby has been born yet."grandma says sarcastically."Go on,enjoy yourself and act like a young lady at all times." Exiting the house as she sits upon the stoop and awaits her girlfriends presence. Chicago,Illinois is their hometown and South Clamiph is where she spent ten years of her life. Her grandmother owns four houses on this block including the one they lived in. All of them two story,brick homes,4 bedrooms, one and a half bath, and basement etc. This is a low income area, alot of poverty stricken folks live out here due to the crime rate, most middle class families rented out their homes and moved to the suburbs of chicago trying to escape reality. However,for whatever reason two to three years later,they were right back where they started from,this is life at its finest. She thought to herself,Why can't i find a job paying thirty to forty thousand a year? It don't make no sense a women like myself with a bachelors degree and advancing myself to a masters degree by next year,out of work. If I don't find a job by next year in any of my fields of learning I'm going to go into a deep state of depression,and never come out the house again. What am I thinking? If they can't see good talent that's too damn bad and it's their lost. I'll start my own business! Thats what I'll do....You go girl! smiling to herself. It was lovely outside,clear skies and a nice smooth breeze.The stars were shining very bright and a beautiful moon lights up the whole world. Marthas heart was at ease and feeling positively energetic about herself,she was ready to let her hair down. However, you have the usuals in the ghetto,friends ,foes,gossipers,drug dealers,player haters,gold diggers,gamblers,addicts,whinos,prostitutes and crack heads. However,none of that stuff took place on her block,which happens to be cleanest block on the southside of chicago. She still was surrounded by murder,mayhem,and misery, the alley ways were filled with horrible acts and terrible scenes. This was the way of life around there that's how come she stayed in school twelve hours a day,to avoid most of the nonsense,and crack was definitely destroying her neighborhood. Ten minutes later Tiffany and Yasha approaches her stoop with matching outfits. Both of them placing their hands upon their hips before saying. "How you like us now!?" Looking extraordinarlly sexy and tasty,drawing lots of attention wearing clear windbreaker jackets by Farah a Corporation thats dominating the clothing market,footwear, music industries,book stores,and etc. They have a unique distinct style and low prices,meeting all the peoples needs. "Girls have yall lost your minds?!"Martha asked,"What?!" t Tiffany barked,"wearing something like dat." "Everyone is watching yall!" "So what,let them look!" "Maybe I can talk some sense into you Yasha because Tiffany is not trying to hear a ting." "Don't waste ya time." Yasha said,"Let's GO!" "I'm not going anywhere with yall until yall change them outfits." snatching her right arm,and pulling her up off the stoop. "Girl we don't have time to change outfits it's twenty after nine."Tiffany whispered harshly. Finally persuading her to come,before kissing on the cheek. A native tradition in their homeland,a form of greeting and or appreciation for one's presence. Guys were watching and speaking,showing no disrespect or any signs of indecency,and all their obscene thoughts they kept to themselves. "Damn yall girls look delicious!"Mark commented " cut it out!'Martha said. Planting smiles on their faces and lust in Yasha's heart. Mark was Danny's best friend and partner in crime, needless to say,Yasha had a crush on him and viceversa on his part. However,his childrens mother was always around,if not close by.She has plenty of eyes in the neighborhood,plus she owns a unisex with 4 floors. Everyones goes to her shop,they do facials,manicures,body massages for adults and teenagers. A game room for the childrens and a movie area for entertainment purposes only.... "Where yall ladies off too?"he asked,"No where in particular,why?" "I was just asking Martha because it's a surprise to see you out this late. You're usually in bed about this time...as a matter of fact ,ain't it pass ya' bed time!" much laughter from everyone. "Are you trying to be funny!" Martha asked, Mark observes that shameful expression on her face from mere embarrasement. He immediately changes that expression and apologizes. "I'm sorry big sis,I didn't mean any harm." "And what are you two laughing at?!"she asked. "It was funny girl," Tiffany said. While still laughing under her breath, however, Yasha immediately stopped and embraced her arm before saying. "Pay her no mind girl.... she's been smoking that stuff." Martha's face lit up before yelling,"What stuff?!!!" " Marijuana girl,Marijuana!" All of a sudden the tables turn and Tifffany became the joke. "Oh so yall wanna start trippin' on me?... I hear dat!" She only speaks her native tongue when she gets emotional. "Are we mad?" Yasha asked, "NO!" Tiffany barked. "Why are we snappin' like dat?!" "Cause yall wanna be actin all crazy." "You got some more of dat stuff?" martha asked "What!....I know you ain't asking for dat!" "Be easy Tiffany before Mark hears you." "Yes i have some more." "MARK, lil bro!" "Yeah,What's up sis?" "Can we sit in your car and listen to some music !?" "Give me a second and I'll toss my keys out the window ." He was in his mother's three story house awaiting an important phone call from his babies mother. Tossing the keys out the window while saying "Don't move my car!" He drove a 1998 navy blue 500 E class mercedes benz stylishly equipped and Martha loved his 12 speaker cd audio system. With 600 watt, amplified subwoofers and digital channels. The car also had, hand selected leather, cross-stitched appointed interior. it was one of the hottest cars in South Chicago and it's color stood out."Girl would you light that stuff already?before he comes downstairs." Martha says. Tiffany lights the joint and passes it to Martha. She took one long pull before passing it to Yasha and started choking.Tiffany patted her on the back several times and her eye's were filled with water. Speaking in a breathless manner, she said "Dat's some powerful shit girl!" "Want some more?" Tiffany asked. "Hold on let me catch my breath." "Take your time when you pull...you don't have to pull that fast and long...check me out!" Tiffany takes nice, long slow drags of the joint."Here!" Martha was definetely a quick learner, however, she still had water in her eyes. "Like dat girl?" she asked, "There you go girl." Tiffany said. Yasha lights the next joint and passes it around. "I'm thirsty and craving for some wine coolers."Yasha said,while licking her lips. "Me too!" "I don't know how my brother smokes dis shit in a blunt."Martha said,They started laughing and everything was moving in slow motion,Martha didn't know if she was coming or going. Their eyes were extremly glossy. Tiffany slides in the hottest cd in town T.L.C. "Damn girl he got all da' latest hits." "Girl my eyes are red ain't they?" Martha asked, nervously and steady looking in the rear view mirror. "Girl will you calm down! you ain't gonna fuck my high up!" Tiffany said. "I don't want Mark to see me like dis!" "Did you bring your shades?" Yasha asked. "Yes!" "Well trow dem' on den'." "How I look?" "Girl if you don't stop it!" "OKAY! OKAY! OKAY!" Yasha just bust out laughing, she couldn't hold it in no more and Tiffany, however, was getting highly upset with them both. "Yasha we ain't gonna start dis' gigglin shit all night!!!!......HOOOO-OOOOOW! Yeah dis is my jammm." Snapping her fingers and bobbing her head to the smooth sounds of T.L.C. " T-Boz is my girl!" she said before turning the music up. Martha immediately turns the music down and yelled at the same time "Girl what da' hell you doing!" "Turning da music up what it look like i'm doin?" "Yasha, please remind me to never get high wit her again!" "I'm just trying to respect his mommas house." "His momma don't live there no more." Yasha whispered. "How do you know?" Martha asked. " We didn't do anyting" "But you was wit him?" "Yes i was, he was polite and respected me to the fullest." "You keepin secrets from me now!!!" Sucking her teeth and rolling her eyes before speaking."PLEASEEEE Tiffany! I told you ,you forgot, smoking so much of dat dirt,it's killing ya brain cells." "I'm sorry baby." "Be quite Tiffany"Martha utters... "Girl did he try you?" "Yes he did, but like i said, he showed me lots of respect." "Why is he knocking on this window?" Martha asked,"Roll da window down and find out." Tiffany said "Yes may we help you?" "Excuse me ladies, a young man upstairs in the third floor window is calling you."" "Thank you sir!" " MARKKK,what is it?" "Turn the damn music up Martha and stop playing games!" "See I told you girl!" Tiffany barked. Turning the music back up while Yasha rollls a joint, and it's a fat one this time. Snapping of the fingers and bobbing of the heads, they were jamming to the beats.

CHAPTER 3

Riding smoothly in his red 1997 jaguar convertible, four seater, xjs, trimmed in gold, while having a deep conversation on his car phone, he acknowledges his gas meters on E and the red lights started flashing. That means he can drive one mile without gas, however, he's four miles away from home and he had to travel through the southside of chicago. Working extra hours today left him exhausted and hungry. The twenty-nine year old Bernard L. Hall, is corporate vice president for Original Style and Original Men Magazine under the publication of FARAH Enterprises. He also owns a modeling agency and clothing store for men, women,and children of all ages. Finally having the opportunity to meet the two owners of FARAH Enterprises today, Raheem and Father. Raheem, the youngest entrepreneurs in the world and being the founder of a prosperous organization gave him strength and power he needed to survive in corporate america. Back on the southside of Chicago .....They were so busy jamming neither of them noticed Mark's presense.(Knocking on the window four times just to get their attention)"Mark,I'm sorry, I didn't hear you." Martha said." Of course not, yall was to busy getting yall grove on....alright were yall want me to drop yall off at because I have some important business to attend to." "The 7-11 on Baker Street." Tiffany said, "Shit yall can walk there!" "Come ooon PLEASE LITTLE BRO, you owe me a ride anyway." Martha mutters," You're absolutely right about that....Hit the back Tiffany and let's go we don't have all day. You need to stop smoking so much of that leaf.You be slow movin like if you got alzheimers disease." Laughs from them all. Dropping them off in front of the 7-11. "Alright here we are and be careful. You need some money Martha?" "Not really but on the other hand I can always use some more." "Here, share this with your click." "May I ask you a question?" "Sure big sis." "How do you feel about Yasha?" "AHH, that's a tough one, you want a lie or the truth?" "You ain't been lying to me and don't start." "I love her dearly." "How long has this been going on?" "Since high school." "That's all I wanted to know" "Here take another hundred and give it to her for me." "You've been taking care of her too,...haven't you?" Shaking his head before saying "Keep this between us and be safe,now be gone, I gotta go." while exiting the Benz, Bernard pulls up right beside them next to the gas pump. Looking at each others cars and giving one another compliments,Bernard speaks first."That's creative and I like it,what year?" "98 and your model?" "It's a 97" Before pulling off mark says:" That's my next car!" Tiffany and yashs already purchased their drinks and told martha she had to get her own. Placing her hands on her curvaceous hips and in a sarcastic manner she said "No problem smart asses, however, I was going to pay for everything." "Girl you know we were just trippin', ain't we hommies for life?"Tiffany asked, "What you take me for....a fool!" much laughter! Waving them away before giving them her back as she walks down the aisle of the convenient store. At this time Bernard walks down the same aisle, noticing an immense heart-shaped back bone and it was bouncing from left to right. Shaking his head while taking a deep breath! he said "DAMN with a ass like that, I can definetly get that lingerie contract from FARAH'sNightwear." Martha reaches for two 40 ounces of Old English and a bottle of Pink Champale. Bernard was in a trance he couldn't believe his eyes, a women so beautiful as herself was drinking 40 ounces. Mesmerized by her figure, complexion, and silky smooth skin. Saying to himself."She's a winner and I ain't seen beauty like that in a while...definately modeling material." Strongly thinking of a way to introduce himself, for he knew he couldn't let such ravishing magnificent beauty vanish right before his eyes.Approaching the counter in such a erotic way,Martha reaches in her back pocket for her money,unconsciously lifting her jersey. A voice from out of nowhere says "DAMMNNNN! Now that's a ASSS!" She thought she heard something, however, not knowing for sure because she was too high. A young man approached her."Excuse Me!" he said "You're

EXCUSED!" Martha says "If you don't mind , I would like to ask you a question." Being very naive she succumbs to his charm, though she was in for a big surprise. "I'm listening." she said. "Is that all you back there?" His eyes were planted directly on her behind. Being so disgusted, however never letting him know and answering his question politely. "Yes I'm afraid so." she said softly speaking. " Now may I ask you a question?" "Yes go right ahead." "Why ya' zipper so tiny?" "Just like your brain! A perfect match and do yourself a favor stop wearing tight jeans...it don't make your dick look any bigger!!!ASSHOLE!". The cashier said out loud,"tell it like it is sister!" Tiffany comes back in the convenient store and in a concern manner she said,"what's the deal girl you alright?" "Yeah i'm alright,I'm just waiting on my change.I broke a hundred dollar bill." "Girl there's this Jaguar outside,you gotta' see it,..It's the bomb!...I wonder who's driving it.' "Find out so we can catch a ride home and go in my bsaement and get tossed." "Are you   crazy!....Not while your Grandma's home." "She's asleep by now,we have nothing to worry about and i'm grown thank you!" "Not too grown for a Traditional spanking." "You aint lying about that." "Here's your change and thanks for having patience." "The pleasure was all mines." Leaving the store and all on their minds,finding that Jaguar driver. Standing at the telephone booths, fronting like if they were using the phones. Bernard immediately approaches the counter,doing his best not to lose sight of martha. Watching,as she turns up the bottle of old English.Giving the cashier a hundred dollar bill before saying,"Sixty dollars on pump two and this friut drink." "Will that be all sir?" "Yes and keep the change." "Are you sure about that?" "Positive,thank you!" "Thank you sir!" Never losing focus on her existence as he exits the store and heads toward the telephone booths. "Excuse me,is anyone using this booth?"Asked Bernard. "No!"Martha said... "OOOO!he's a cuty!" "Don't mind her"...Martha said nicely,"stop that Tiffany,we are suppose to be looking for the Jaguar driver." Bernard had a car phone however,going out of his way to get her attention and doing whatever needed to be done to capture her spirit. Yasha was using the telephone for real. "Girl who you talking to." "None of your business nosey!" Slamming the booth's door with a huge smile on her face.Tiffany couldn't believe what she just did to her. "Ahh,poor baby look at your face,"Martha mutters. Did you see what she did to me?Tiffany cried. "You know she's in love." "All i wanted to know was, who's she's talking to." "It's Mark." "Word!" "I kid you not." "He's going to end up leaving his children's mother for her." "I know and she deserve it because when him and my brother was locked up,she was busy running around cheating on him...Missing plenty of visits,after seeing my brother,i would call him down and encourage him to keep his head together..His mother would bring the children up because they wasn't on good terms,for the last two years of his bid." "I got something to tell you..." "What is it!?" Tiffany had this strange look upon her face. "I must confess!..I use to bring her with me every time i go see your brother and she would visit Mark." "So what!....that's no reason to confess." "I wasn't finish yet...One day we were visiting them and she showed up with his kids." "So what happened!?" "she showed her ass and they put her out along with the children.I don't know why she was mad,..She was cheating on him then." Bernard staring her down,meditating about how he would love to be her personal photographer and Agent.His thoughts grew deeper,how about a guarantee contract with my boss or the owners of FARAH ENTERTAINMENT....And i know for sure she can make covergirl for our magazines.We need new faces and models,she's at the top of the line,knocking all other models out the box. I gotta get her attention and now is the time. Martha feels this strange vibe,like if someone was watching her. "Tiffany, come here." "what?" "Is that man looking at me?" "Hell yeah,he aint took his eyes off of you yet." "I felt someone eyes on me." "He's cute!"Tiffany commented. "I know,but i'm trying to ride around tonight..I aint with all this walking stuff." "Girl let me find out that thing is hot." "Hot aint the word." "Martha,now you know thats the alcohol talking!" Bernard immediately interveins,"Excuse me young ladies,would anyone care to assist me with some directoins?" "Where you trying to go?"Tiffany shouted. I need to find Highway 95south." "O' that won't be a problem." That's all he wanted to do,was strike a conversation. "Excuse my rudeness the name's Bernard." "Hi Bernard,and excuse our rudeness.This Yashsa,Martha and my name is Tiffany but you can call me Tiff." "What are you girls doing tonight?" "O' nothing,the usual...hanging out,catching some breeze and enjoying ourselves." Martha wasn't paying him any mind although Tiffany's flirtatiousness was a part of her nature,loving attention. Steady drinking was Martha and watching that Jag. "Excuse me Tiffany...I would like to say something to your friend,if you don't mind." "O' go right ahead." Touching Martha's shoulder and getting her attention. Startling her causing her to jerk back while dropping her 40 oz. He immediately apologizes and offers to buy her a real drink,she accepts the offer. Their eyes meet and before they knew it they felt immediate attraction for each others. Noticing her eyes wondering over at his Jag a few times,in a respectable manner he asked,"That's a beautiful car aint it?" "Yes it is!"Martha whispered softly. "I observed you glancing at it a few times." "It's just so pretty." "Do you have license?" "Unfortunately i don't." "Would you like to go for a ride in it?" "i don't mean no harm when i say this,...I'm trying to find the owner now." "What if i told you ,your speaking with the owner." "OOH' i feel so embarrassed!"Placing her hand over her mouth. "Don't be,come.." "Is it alright if my friends ride with us?" "i don't have a problem with that." "IT's not that i don't trust you or anything,...It's just the girls night out and i don't want for you to think we're using you as a chauffeur." "I don't mind chauffeuring a gorgeous woman like you around." "You're so nice,and i truly thank you for the compliment." "Youwelcome!" Blushing like she just recieved a kiss from her secret admire,chills swimming threw her blood from mere excitement. Thoughts creeping in her mind. He's sooo cute,respectful,polite and charming,however trusting him takes time and tolerance. Grandma's saying,respect and trust,now i understand what she meant by that. Love over night,not at first sight,..That's something we must fight and it's a on going flight. I wonder what my brother's doing,he hasn't beeped me all night.   Back at the garage and cap stand.... " Go do what you do best, make sure you cover your tracks and we'll talk tomorrow alright..PEACE!" "Danny!" "YO!" " Mikasa said,When you gonna send a ride for her?" "Damn, I forgot!....you busy?" "Nah" " Do the honors Mike, I got you when you get back." "Alright!" "This is our last set right?" Danny asked "Yeah!" Benching six fifty with broad shoulders and chest. Danny was a true workaholic when it came to working out. Strenuous weightlifting, push-ups, pull-ups, and his favorite, sit-ups, one thousand a clip. Danny's weight 180 pounds solid, height 6'1", complexion dark brown and jet black curly hair. "Finish, I'm outta here, show time." Danny yelled!.. "No Doubt!" "See you in three days." "Two man,Two!" "Oh Yeah that's right, this the fourth week."   Doing 85 on the highway, trying to impress Martha to the fullest. Tiffany and Yasha in the back jamming to the smooth sounds of Babyface. "Go Girl!" Tiffany yells, "HOOO! NOOO!YOOO!" Tiffany don't play games when it comes to partying, being the loosest one out of the group left her very vulnerable. However, knowing this didn't change her ways and actions. Bernard stares in his rear -view mirror at Tiffany and Yasha, saying to himself. "They look good too, but not as good as Martha. Tiffany has a big set of boobs, definetly swim suit material and Yasha's tawny smooth skin with that sweet little baby face and green eyes. Where have these girls been all my life? I think I'mma visit the ghettoes more often." Starting to feel more comfortable around Bernard, glancing at him every chance she gets. He noticed her beautiful eyes were checking out his physique, however he didn't want to make the wrong move and business was first. Tiffany removes her jacket and starts bouncing around to the smashing sounds of Mary J's new single. Innocently glimpsing in his rearview mirror and to his surprise Tiffany's breast were wobbling vivaciously. Whispering to himself," She looks marvelous in that zebra bikini top, let me guess a 37D or 38D, it's either one or the other. I can see her now in the latest swimsuits, sports brassiere, the newest designs out and FARAH bikini wear. Man I have, three million dollar projects in my possession, all I have to do is play my cards right and B.L.H modeling agency needs new taste."

One hour later.......

"Mr. Stewart everything is done." "Good looking out Rick, how much do I owe you?" "One thousand seven hundred and fifty dollars." "Hrer you go and keep the change." "I appreciate this Mr. Stewart." "It's no sweat Rick, you do a great job around here you deserve it." Rick leaves with joy in his heart and Danny was well pleased with his work. He's the best mechanic in town, a very well loved man with no kids, no wife and most of his family is dead, it's just him and his father. Danny goes to get his dogs out the basement, taking them for a walk in his parking lot. Awaiting his girlfriend's presence the long love of his life and I must say she's very sexy. Walking slowly through his lot playing with both bulldogs with a two by four. Someone softly called out his name, turning around to locate that sexy voice. There stood Mikasa, 39C, 23, 36, height 5'8" 125 pounds, hair in one long ponytail reaching her lower back. Wearing an all black round neck sleeveless body fitted long skirt with side slits to her thighs, and leather black round ankly sandals. Her skin a glowing light brown the same color as her eyes. One large diamond choker chain worth sixty-five thousand dollars, with a matching bracelet, anklet, watch,and twin rings worth two hundred thousand dollars. She's a upcoming recording artist under FARAH Records. Growing up in church the one Danny's grandmother brought two years ago. Winning the first place prize this year and walking away with a check for a half a million dolllars plus a two year contract under FARAH Records. She's the first gospel singer to ever win in the original style talent show. However loving her first man and sex partner for over five years and putting up with all his non-sense, in and out of jail, sleeping around, you name it, he's doing it. Being taught by her mother to stick by her man no matter what, that's because she was a gold digger herself, always chasing that mighty dollar. "I thought we was going out to dinner?" Mikasa guffed. "I had some important business to take care off and don't give me that sorryful look." "What sorryful look?" she barked. "Can I get a kiss before you get highly upset?" "Highly upset ain't the word, more like fed up!" "Look woman! I told you I had some important business to take care of!" "You always have some important business to take care of!" "And what's that supposed to mean?" " Everytime it's our day to spend together, yo' behind always got something sooo important to do....keep it up Danny, you'll see!!!!" " I know you ain't threating me, that's for one, and I asked for you to come give me a kiss! that's two." Glaring at him before walking between his legs and giving him that kiss. In a snarly manner she said, "You wanna see my bad side don't you?" "NO!" he replied desirably, "You know I love you Mikasa more than life itself." Gripping her buttocks, massaging them firmly and kissing all over her breast. "STOP!" she said in a scornful tone,as she feels this negative vibe. Not wanting to tell him that the owner of FARAH Entertainment took her out to dinner about three hours ago and things got a little heated in his limo,though it wasn't all his doing. "Why are you acting like that?" he asked. "I don't know Danny!?" turning her back on him and folding her arms tightly as to secure herself. How could she explain to him that she allowed another man to fondle with her vagina and caress her breast, never wanting to stop him, and enjoying every minute of it. Being treated like a real woman for the first time, opening of the doors, pulling out the chairs and paying more attention to her needs then anything else. Thinking to herself. Here is a man two years younger than I, who owns a enterprise spends three hours with me without any interruptions. On the other hand, here's a man I've been with for five years the same age. Three of those five years I did with him while he was in prison, still cheating on me and I can't even get a hour of his time without any interruptions unless it envolves sex..... "I know you hear me talking to you!" he barked, being very angry and ready too tear her head off. "Don't you ever turn your back on me again BITCH!" Pulling her ponytail and wrapping his huge arms around her neck. Forcefully whispering in her ear,"Don't let that singing contract go to your head!" "You're hurting me baby." she cries. "This is what you like!....Coming in here with that stinky ass attitude." she was terrified of him,However, patiently awaiting to escape his presence, this time for good and never coming back. "You gonna take you're ass in that office and relax until daddy's ready to leave....understand?" "Yes baby" she replies fearfully. Releasing her from his tight grip and slapping her on the ass real hard. Tears in her eyes and hatred in her heart, abusing this woman phsically, mentally, and spiritually. Doing exactly what he said and thinking to herself."He's History tonight!, I'mma hire me two bodyguards and take out an order of protection. I can't keep taking all this abuse especially the physical drama...I'm to damn young for this shit!"

CHAPTER 4

At the bar inside of the FARAH Hotel...Showing identification to get in , unfortuantly Martha didn't meet their dress requirements.Never the less Bernard had carteblanche keeping everybody happy.The place was glamourous with 4bars,4dance floors and the second floor had male and female strippers live entertainment. everyone takes a seat as the waitress approaches their section. "care to oder?"she asked. None of the girls knew what to ask for,Bernard recognizes this and oders for everyone,to save embarrassment. "are yall still serving the appetizer?"he asked. "Yes sir!" "I like four appetizers,a bottle of grand marnier margarita and a bottle of FARAH dry champagne.O' i almost forgot,I would like a chalice to drink from." "Will that be all Mr.Hall?" "Yes,thank you." Tiffany was bobbing to the music and Yasha wanted to dance, badly.Their wishes were answered by two twin brothers,who were professional models from Bernard's Agency. "Hey Mr.Hall." "How's it going twins?" "alright couldn't be better." "Excuse my rudeness,Trevor and Travis this is Martha,Tiffany and Yasha some friends of mines." Glancing at Tiffany,poor Travis mesmerized by those zebra bikini tops,stood out giving them that young and tender look. Tiffany steady bobbing her head and snapping her fingers feeling the music. Finally gaining enough courage,Travis askes Tiffany while reaching for her hand for a dance,.. She accepts. Trevor whispered in Yasha's ear. Smiling while slowly rising with excitement as he escorted her to the dance floor. Reaching for Martha's hand ebulliently hoping for her acceptance and overflowing grace. Martha didn't know how to receive his invitation,nor his charming embrace,although a strong vibration travels threw her blood and her heart palpitates. A slow song comes on and he askes her in a glamorous manner,"Would you like to dance?" Cheerfully answering him,"Yes!" Hugging all over the twins were Tiffany and Yasha enjoying themselves.... Rapping her arms around his neck,as he raps his arms around her waist,moving slowly and bodies touching. Never letting a man get this closer to her ever. Brushing up against his bulky chest,her bosom and wanting to palm her curvaceous bodacious booty,never the less maintaining his composure and controlling those weaker desires in oneself. Feeling different about herself,not knowing if she was moving to fast or to slow though,cocksure about his trust.Being a virgin left her a bit shaky in that department and he would definitely have to be patient,hence it will be worth the wait. A 25 year old virgin with a delicate smooth body,no bruises,no stretch marks nothing but pure beauty and one of GOD's finest creation,mentally,physically and spiritually. That's a gift for a man,the best gift in the world. Wanting to give her a kiss,however he waits and wanting him to kiss her before it's to late...Looking straight into her eyes before saying,"you're so beautiful inside and out,...I would like the opportunity to spend more time with you,if thats alright?" Not knowing what to say,allowing her heart to lead her and speaking in a low sexy tone,"I don't have a problem with us getting to know one another." Giving him this powerful sensual look."kiss me!"she muttered. Eagerly with out hesitation,and wanting very much to taste those plumb juice lips of hers.Thinking to himself,is there not anything on this woman's body thats not plumb? Closing her eyes awaiting his energetic touch.Their lips meet and tonques unite.A great feeling of ecstasy flows threw her body and a tingling sensation touches her vulva.The night's just begun,the moon is full and lots of prophecies will be fulfilled. Who knows what will happen,life has its promising opportunity and spell binding event.

CHAPTER 5

Bernard's studio was crowded, women all over the place, beauty everywhere and no one's dissatisfied. Photographers's setting up for work with photo assistance near by. "What's taking them so long?" Bernard inquired. "I hope she didn't forget, I told her two weeks from now." His cell phone buzzes. "Yeah!" "Excuse me Mr. Hall there are three lovely young ladies standing before me. They claim they have an appointment, however, it's not on record." "I'm sorry my precious secretary, I forgot to note that in your book. Let them up, I"ve been exspecting them." "Go right ahead girls, to the left and take these passes so security won't bother you." Their bodies were tensed, and Martha was tentative about modeling underwear, however, Yasha and Tiffany were excited about the whole matter. The stairs to the second floor had marble floors what a beautiful sight. "I'm not sure about this girls," Martha said with this doubtful expression. "Come on Martha!" Yasha said "Everything will be allright, it's three of us." Tiffany paying them no mind, reaches the top of the steps, "What are yall waiting for, come on," she grumbled. "Martha this is our only chance to get out the ghetto, on our own....Please don't ruin this opportunity for us. Besides if they get stupid in there, I got my blade girl and I will cut somebody to short to shit." Martha takes a deep breath. "I'm ready," she said. Tiffany opens the door and to their surprise, women all over the place some half dressed, and other 's naked. Cameras, Lights, and painted sceneries you name it, they had it. "Yes may we help you?" The doorman asked. "Yes we have an apppointment with Mr. Hall," Martha said nervously. Making his way to the dooor was Bernard. "Hey, what took yall so long?" I had to reschedule yall.... But don't worry, we can still get some photos shots of you, come!" Tiffany couldn't believer her eyes tits and ass everywhere and no one seems to care. Yasha on the other hand was stunned by the extravagant designs, which gave the place a marvelous look. "You two go with this lady and Martha you go with Mrs. Allred, the number 1 fashion designer in the city." "How do you do Martha?" "Fine Mrs.Allred." "You look a bit nervous, don't be, however it's natural for new comers." Entering a big room with a large heart shaped jacuzzi, on the otherside was this forest scenery with two large rock and a small waterfall between them. Mrs. Allred wheels over a clothing rack filled with the latest designs by FARAH, Giorgio Armani, Marc Jacobs, John Gallino, and Tommy Hillfiger. "You will dress from this rack," Mrs. Allred said, "Relax young lady your going to be with us for a couple of hours so put this robe on." "Ohh it's beautiful!" Martha said,"Can I keep it?" "I don't see why not you'll be the only one using it. Let's go we don't have all day." "Where can I change at?" "Behind the blinds darling." "Mrs. Allred, will he be watching me?" "Sweetheart don't worry, he's your photographer and he's only here to do his job."

Bernard walks over to the garden and beach scenery. There stood Yasha with an all burgundy satin strapless gown, looking extremely sexy. Her measurements was 38c -22 - 35, height 5'7", 120 pounds, tawny complexion, light brown eyes, jet black hair, and a cute little babyface,21 years old. Saying to himself, "That million dollar smile and those gorgeous hips, will do it everytime." Tiffany comes out wearing a silk mustard bikini set with her chocolate complexion, hazel eyes, jet black hair, and a trunk that was well stacked. Her measurements were 37d-24-38,height 5'8", 130 pounds, and definitely a ebony babe,24 years old. Whispering to himself. "I wonder if Travis taste that yet?" "Excuse me Mr. Hall." "Yes Tony." "Mrs. Allred said, she ready for you." "Okay, Thank you!" Making his way towards his private modeling room, opening the door slowly. Martha was striking poses like a natural in a lime green snake print top by FARAH. Crochet Bikini bottoms by Bantu-Farah. "Uh-Huh I see you," Bernard said. Giving him this sexy glimpse before smiling, However, continuing with her work, changing her outfit to a more sexier one. Coming out in the latest swimsuit, a lavender velvet strapless bikini set by Negus - Farah. "MMM, yummy," he mutters. Her measurements, 35d-24-37, height 5'9", 127 pounds, a golden brown complexion, jet black hair hanging below her shoulders and dark brown almond shaped eyes, only 25 years old. Thinking to himself. She's beyond a shadow of a doubt, the beautifullest women I've ever seen and I've seen alot. I want her for myself and if it takes settling down she's worth it. Changing in this third outfit, which was a maroon trapeze cocktail dress silk chiffon and bantu negus sandals. Strutting down the walkway with this striking appearance, and buttocks just wobbling like jello. Starting to feel sexy, enjoying herself to the fullest and her breast stood at attention. The CEO, of Original Men and Original Style Magazines walks in. "Good Day," Bernard said. "Like wise son, and who's that lovely young lady?" "That's my new project Mr. Handley." " I see you have alot of ebony babes this week...I want her on the front cover of Original Men Magazine, and the two out front, sugar and spice makes the front cover of Original Style Magazine, next month's issues...what's their price?" "I don't yet Mr. Handley,but before the nights out I can have a price for you." Bernard whispered. "You do that! just remember, I want them first before the wolves come out! Understand?" "Yes, Mr. Handley sir." He pats Bernard on the shoulder before leaving the room silently. That's his way of saying you've just earned yourself a raise.

"OPEN THE DOOR NOW!!!!! YOU STUPID LITTLE BITCH,"Danny Barked. "Please Danny leave, it's over!!!! I DON'T LOVE YOU ANYMORE!!!!!" Mikasa screams. He runs around back, jumping the fence, and kicks the backdoor in. She immediately runs to the phone, unfortunately he beats her to it. Sadly her mother was out of town handeling some important real estate business. Purchasing a mini-mansion worth 900,000 thousand dollars in Pikesvill, Maryland. Doing her best to escape the cruel hands of her first lover. "WHY YOU HAVEN'T BEEN RETURNING MY CALLS BITCH!!!!!?" In his eyes was the sight of darkness she didn't know what to say, fearing for her life, and never taking her eyes off of him. Hoping somebody would hear his harsh voice. Taking small steps back, as he forces himself. "GET OFF OF ME!" She yells. Paying her no mind before saying," YOU DON'T LOVE ME ANYMORE BITCH?" She ignores him not wanting to say the wrong thing. He tries to kiss her, moving her face from side to side. Grabbing her jaw and forcefully sticking his tongue down her throat. Ripping her clothes off, and in a scroudrel manner he said,"You brought this on yourself bitch!" "You don't have to do this to me,please." she cried. He gets worst, continuing with his abusive treatment and his anger grew rampantly. Trying her best to fight him off with tears in her eyes and resentment in her heart. Taking what didn't belong to him anymore, feeling him inside of her left her breathless and ashamed. This was inappropriate and he knew it, though he didn't care holding her mouth as he pumps away. Biting his hand, scratching his neck, face, and chest. Doing whatever it takes to protect herself, being violated to the fullest left her no choice. He started punching her, spitting on her, and ramming himself inside her savagely. Stuttering, while screaming in great pain for help after he realeses his evil nature inside of her, he gets up kicking her several times before leaving out the front door. She could barely move, in great pain,nevertheless, making it to the phone to call for help before fainting.

"Break time Martha," Mrs. Allred yells.Putting her hot pink robe on before walking in Bernard's direction.Giving her a kiss on her cheek before saying,"I have some great news for you my dear." So anxious to hear what he had to say and wanting to know if he was well pleased with her modeling skills. Not giving him her full attention after saying,"Thank you for everything Bernard." "You don't have to thank me,you're the professional around here. All i did was supply you with the material and a very important person was checking you out...Wanting you to be the cover girl on next month's issue of Original Men Magazines." "you wouldn't be pulling my leg would you?" "Hell no!...Original Men Magazine is one of the famous magazines in the world." Her eyes expanded from mere excitement, hugging all over bernard in tears. "You did it baby,"he said cheerfully. "I did,didn't I!" "Watch this, Mrs. Allred!" "Yes, Mr. Hall." "Is she worthy of a million bucks?" Spinning her around twice. "Yes, she is." answered Mrs. Allred." Then a million bucks it is. How you like to work for her full-time.?" "If she can afford my salary cap...The pleasure would be all mines." "What's the cap?" Martha asked. "250 thousand a year." "What!" martha barked, "I don't have that type of money honey." Laughter fills the room. "Who's her agent?" Mrs. allred inquired. "Why me of course." "Well if you're her agent Mr. Hall I know she can afford me." "Here, take this card and mrs. Allred will assist you.Spend no less than 500 thousand dollars....I'll see you tomorrow, I have some contract deals to make.Oh, how could i forget, take your friends with you and here's they keys to one of my condos, it's a gift from me to you it's already fully furnished." She didn't know what to say,Consequently hugging him once again and throwing her tongue in his mouth, Surprising him, though hugging her back, swallowing all of her saliva while moving his hands slowly below her waist and down her hips. She knew he wanted to rub her ass, grabbing his hands and placing them on her rump. "Awesome!" he whispered. Thinking to himself, soft like a sponge and shaped like a heart, definitely a juicy booty, voluptuous. Squeezing softly..rubbing slowly and her breast pressed up against his bulky chest feeling like nice sized water baloons. Arousing him to the fullest as well as herself, pulling back the both of them , and apologizing too each other for they knew they went too far. In a sexy manner she said."I'll see you tomorrow." Slowly walking away blowing him air kisses and waving good night.Before exhaling.

Being so disgusted with herself for not telling the police who really assalted her and never mentioning the sexual abuse. Her mother immediately comes home after hearing the attack on her daughter. Comforting her in her time of need however never questioning her about the situation for she knew exactly who done this. The doctor examines her, noticing that she was sexually abused. In an unpleasant manner she said."Don't utter a word of this to anyone, do you hear me!" "Yes ma'am." Telling him, "It wasn't rape it was hard sex." Her mother enters the room and in a uppity voice she spoke."His ass is mines!Do you hear me!? all mine, and your mini- mansion is ready. I'm packing up, we are leaving today, and your agent called. He said you can work in their studio in Maryland." "Why you didn't let me speak with him?" she blurted. "Baby your not in any position to be speaking to anyone. Anyway he's in africa, and he's sending you two bodyguards, martial arts experts free of charge."He's so sweet momma." " Yes i know you, however, you should be focusing on completing your album." "Please momma that's my least worry." "And what is your greatest?" "That damn Danny!" wrapping her arms around her shoulders holding her real tight and shedding tears the both of them.

"That jamaican piece of shit thinks he's untouchable. I'm tired of his shit man," kibbles said. "Fuck this turf shit he ain't even from america.... I'm born and raised here! How the hell he gonna tell me where I can come and go." "He's right, that Danny is getting a little bit beside himself. Plus if we get rid of him we'll be doing the community a favor." killer raved. "I hear you two very clearly." Kane grumbled, "I don't break treaties unless someone violates." "He violated!" kibbles shouted. "What do you mean?" kane asked. "He was with my cousin last night." "What you talking about?" "She's been seeing him on numerous occasions. He don't want us fucking with any of his bitches. Like that badass sister of his, he damn near had a heart attack two weeks ago....when i tried to slide my dick up in her." Guffas from each of them. "Yeah I must say she's one fine ass bitch," killer whispered, "I bet that pussy is tight and wet, throbbing for penetration. Last week at Jackson's pool, wearing this white bathing suit..I was awarded the opportunity to watch that fat pussy breathe." "I like to hear this one," kane said impulsively. Killer clears his throat before saying," She dives in the pool swimming across slowly with swift strokes, arriving at the end , climbimg out and resting in her beach chair along with two of her best friends. Legs wide opened and you know me binoculars steady focusing. Raising her right leg while lotioning her thigh, getting a direct clear focus of that hairy cunt, and i kid you not...it was talking to me." "What did it say?" kibbles muttered. "I'm in jail break me out! and I promise you I'll be your good slave." Much laughter. "Hahahahaha!! Man your fuckin crazy!" kane outbursted. "That's my word! I heard it talking ,and yall know she's a virgin.... never been touched, so whoever breaks that ice ain't gonna be able to get rid of her. Trust me when i tell you."

Escorted by four bodyguards from BLH Agency, and riding comfortably in a chauffeur driven limo grey mercedes benz, complimentary of the agency. "stop here!" Mrs. Allred shouted, in the car's intercom. This was the biggest foreign dealership in the state of illinois. "okay girls, first things first, you have to have cars to go with those beautiful appearences of yours. There's nothing like a foreign car...when you're desplaying such beauty as yourselves. As your fashion designer, I will tell you what to wear, and what not to wear. What to eat and what not to eat.Where you should hangout and where you shouldn't hangout.What company to keep and what company to get rid of ,needless to say your dating habits should stay in the realms of your ability to prosper...Don't stare at me like that,this is what i get paid to do. If you need anyone to consult too,just think of me as your second mother...I keep secrets understand?...now you can be the most successful woman in the business,but you have to be very observant and never sell yourself cheap, at anytime..! Men will try to sleep with you, rich men,Bourgeoisie men,single and or married men,promising you the world.A word from the wise,Don't trust them...Business first and pleasure last....now lets go purchase three cars of your choice, and we don't have all day,we have other shopping to do. "

   Sitting in his condominiun with two naked women,Lesbians from the boulevard. Around the way girls who were all about money and love the finset things in life.Drinking Moet and smoking marijuana while watching sexy Sabrina shake her ass to the smooth sounds of R.Kelly. 32D,26,40, hight 5'10 weighing 165pounds with hazal eyes long brown hair and this golden complexion. A star with irresistible presence in a world of eccentrics and being the wildest around the way.Natalie on the other hand was the submissive one with huge breast and soft skin very delicate like a babies ass. 44D,26,38,brown hair,dark brown eyes,height5'9,159pounds,a dark chocolate complexion and a wet hot twat. Doing what she does best,besides fucking him,massaging his shoulders and chest. Reminiscing about that abuse he'd done earlier to his future.Loving her to much, turned him into a mad man,and he knew this. "Sit on this dick,Danny barked. "Yes dady!"Sabrina whispered."You don't have to scream,mommy's here to please you." Sliding down on his penis simultaneously jerking in motion as she squeezes her vigina muscles .Natalie's feeling herself while massages his neck with her massive tits and hard like peanuts her nipples stood erect. Heating up that desire inside of him and loving every minute of it creating a strong sensation. Gripping Sabrina's humongous black booty. "fuck my tight pussy!.."Sabrina moans. Bouncing even more frantically on his bonner,until he exploded from mere moistness and friction. "Oh,baby cum in me please!!!..she yells.

   Bernard, relaxing in his crush velvet recliner,inside his 2.5millon dollar mansion in Springfield Illinois. Receiving on his fax machine,the point home network intel computer system,seven contracts from different corporations and organizations. Four magazine contracts worth five million dollars,two TV.commercials and one cosmetic contract worth four million dollars. Saying to himself,"I've just made nine-million big ones with my internet...My email hasn't stop yet,I'mma call it a night...Should i call her before i lie down?..Nah,I'mma let her enjoy herself, i don't wanna come on to fast."

CHAPTER 6   TWO YEARS LATER JUNE 21,1999.........

People are preparing for the next millennium, technology is at it's finest reproduction and politics, doing what they do best,NOTHING!!!!

   Cruising down the highway laid back listening to Debra Cox in her brand new red drop top FERRARI F-355, complimentary from FARAH ENTERPRISE. Wearing a red velvet mini skirt and sports bra by Bantu Farah, with matching sandals by Negus Farah. Signing a five year contract, after winning the SUPER MODEL OF THE YEAR AWARD from Farah Designs, her accalades from commercials and magazines made her worth twenty-two million dollars. Purchasing two homes one in Kingston, Jamaica and Pikesville, Maryland. Each worth 1.4 million dollars.Parked in her many garages were 4 vehicles from FARAH DEALERSHIP 1999 models: a green dodge viper, a yellow lotus espirit, a gold mercedes benz E 55 and a dark brown jeep land rover suv. Her versatility and charisma opened many doors for her. Gaining the public's eye helped to launch her new acting career. Appearing on four sitcoms, three talk shows, three music videos, and two HBO specials, which she displayed an outstanding performance. Starring in her first premiere motion picture coming soon called: "DEEPER THAN MY GRAVE". Her business status was great owning four boutiques back at home, two beauty salons in Chicago, and a restaurant in Maryland. That's not all being CEO of S and S Modeling Agency which was owned by her best friends Yasha and Tiffany. This agency was located in Kingston,Jamaica their homeland. Yasha and Tiffany expanded their modeling careers also going to Europe and dominating the fashion industy under the title, Sugar and Spice. Also receiving a five year contract from FARAH Enterprise. Not only did they owned a major modeling agency out of the Country. They owned a four story athletic fitness club in Chicago. Finally having the opportunity to fufill their dreams, moving their parents out of the ghetto and donating one million dollars to restructure condemned homes and community centers in their old neighborhood. The greatest fufillment was that double wedding they had six months ago, worth three hundred thousand dollars. Yasha married Mark her ghetto king and tiffany married Travis the top Twin model from BLH Agency. There was lots of money being made between the three of them. However Martha was still single and enjoying every minute of it. She accumulated in two years twenty-five million dollars. Buying her brother a porsche carrera last month, after bailing him out of jail. Trying her best to get him to go back home with their grandmother, he's hooked on this american life. He was out of control and there was nothing she could do, loving her only brother kept her focused. Arriving one hour late for a very important photo session. "You're late young lady," Mrs. Allred said. "I'm sorry, I lost track of time,"Martha rants. "What's the matter?" "It's that time of the month and my stomach is killing me." "We can cancel the session due to the fact that nature is calling." "Nah, let's get this over with." "areyou sure?" Mrs. Allred asked concerned. "Yes momma, I'm sure." Mrs. Allred leaves her dressing room yelling at the top of her lungs. "Let's go people we don't get paid to sit on our asses and drink coffee all day.My baby will be ready in ten minutes." Setting up and taking their positions one photographer said to another,"You ain't seen nothing yet freshman." "What?"corey blurted. "Feast your eyes on this,"Randy whispered lustfully.

Strutting down the runway in a sleevelesss roundneck snake-skin body suit by Jaquetta Lanee' Farah and sandals by Bantu Farah. The audience was amazed at such beauty, quietly snapping pictures and the commentators couldn't say anything bad about this hot diamond. "WOW!" Slowly leaving the runway applause from everyone. Two men approaches the runway from Vataz Enterprise they wanted martha to run their communications department. Offering her top dollar but being dedicated to Bernard and Farah Enterprise turns them down. Bernard takes a seat at the end of the runway so he can get a excellent look at his employee and friend. Wanting her so bad, however, she's playing hard to get. She wants to get married before having sex, he on the other hand didn't want to get married claiming he's to young and so was she. Silence fills the air as everybody awaits her return. Never letting her fans down,sashshaying in a ostentatious manner down the runway. eyes stretched, hearts pounded and jaws dropped even Bernard was astonished. Wearing a sheer white v-neck Trenae' Octavia sheath gown.Worn over a black velour lace Bra and panties set.Silver sandals by Negus Farah. Light steady flashing from the cameras, slow long bobs from the chinese spectators. Spinning thrice before making it to the end of the runway.Noticing her agent's expression,"Pick your jaw up,"she whispers,after throwing him a big kiss. Smiling was the suave and handsome debonair,agent Bernard. Wanting badly to sex her brains out,however,insisting on a commitment first before anyman gets to taste her jewels. If this wasn't enough to change his mind,nothing will. "A commitment you want then it's a commitment you will get,"Bernard said Ingenuously. He couldn't take it anymore,two years of lustful thoughts,frantic desires and sleepless night. Looking so ravishing, as she strides back down the runway. The twenty three year old successful Entrepreneur,owner and C.E.O. of FARAH Enterprise, enters the auditorium. Styling a green rayon Taffeta vest with matching trousers by Negus Farah and supple suede green oxfords with Lug soles by Bantu Farah. A platium Movado watch coverd with Diamonds,matching Braclet and pinky rings,rocks just glittering strong enough to blind a bull. Being escorted by four huge body guards,African brothers from Nairobi Kenya. Bernard immediately greets him,"So glad you could make it Raheem." "So am i. " Taking a seat before saying,"Where's our drop dead beauty?" "She'll be out in ten minutes,"Bernard responded dryly. At this time one of the guards goes out to the limo to get the two dozens of roses. Father walks in,a much older man,very intelligent and business minded. He's C.O.O. of FARAH Enterprise,handling all advertisement,multimedia systems and finances. "Sorry im late brother Rah." "Don't sweat it,i was late myself." "Here you go brother Raheem." Handing him the roses before standing on guard. "Are those for the lovely young super model?"Father asked. "yes,indeed." "She will be delighted to meet you two,for the first time,"Bernard said. "Sounds as if our feelings are mutual,"Father commented. "What are they doing here?"Raheem asked politely. These were his unqualified competitors,Vataz enterprise. They were always trying to buy out his contracts and steal his employees. "Don't start,we don't own this place, and it is a fashion show...If you purchase tickets you can get in,"Father responded seriously. "I know those cut throats already offered my Supermodel lots of money...I'll tell you this much,if they try to buy her contract out,I'll triple their offer,"he said boisterously. "Don't worry Mr.Raheem,...she's going nowhere,"Bernard commented. Returning to the runway was our lovely sexy supermodel. Wearing a body fitting sleeveless Mandarin-style Negus Gown,showing that bodacious curvaceous heart shaped ass,she very well possessed. Her bust looked like two medium size melons with nipples the size of thumbs. She's definitely a box ofice hit and doing what she does best, erotically moving with this exotic glow. 95% of the men in the audience adulated her beauty, and figure. A handful of spectators were bowing with appreciation. "she looks marvelously expensive,"Father spoke joyfully. However Raheem couldn't speak, being mesmerized by her posture,her elegance and the way she moved with such genuineness. stopping infront of Raheem,not recognizing who he is,due to the excessive flashing of the lights. However, noticing those roses and sweet smelling fragrance. Raheem stood eagerly giving her this romantic stare while handing her the roses. Kneeling too accept her gift,their hands touch and a strong sensation travels through their bodies. Slowly kissing her hand before releasing it and to his surprise, kissing him on the cheek. Bernard thought nothing of it because she does that too all of her fans who gives her flowers. Though he didn't know that she was one of Raheem's biggest fans. Wanting to know how he became so successful at a young age,being born and raised in the worse part of the Ghettoes of Chicago. She had no idea who he was, never having the opportunity to meet him until now and not being aware of it. Her quick success lured him closer to her,watching videos of her while on vacation in Africa for a year,learning the arts of battle by a dear friend and advisor. With this erogenous feeling, as she walks back down the runway with those lovely roses in her arms, beautiful back shots of her buttocks bouncing from side to side. Our single C.E.O. was thinking to himself.' A vacation just me and her for about two or three weeks. looking just like the sisters in the Mother land,Sexy,healthy and extremely luscious... I'mma take my time with this one, I'll let her come to me,..That's exactly what I'll do.' Having a intimate relationship with solo recording artist Mikasa William taught him alot about sexy women,who's resemblance was of a Goddess. Departing with out any hostilities although, the over night success went to her head. In two years time, three platinum albums,two glod singles,co-staring in two movies. Receiving one black Achievement award, and one soul train music award. Appearing on the front cover of Original Style, and Farah Magazines. Wanting him in her presence twenty four hours a day, not going to happen,he had a Enterprise to run. Being so stubborn and possessive lead to their departure. Giving her five million dollars to keep her mouth closed,no media talk. Friends not enemies, still in love,although sneaking off every now and then,calling him several times a week. He was her first true love and she was heart broken,blaming herself for their separation. Going in to a deep state of depression,and having a nervous break down. Coming to her aid and assuring her, that it's not her fault. Apologizing for her ways and actions,letting him know that she didn't mean to treat him like her ex-boyfriend treated her. Maintaining her insanity and that's only because he sleeps with her every now and then. No man has ever treated her like Raheem,and loving him so much regreting the loss. Danny was plotting and scheming on the eastside murderers. Receiving threats while incarcerated made him vengeful. Acting out his m.o agian,sexually and physically assulting one of the gange members cousin. Dating Natalie for eight months before committing such cruel acts.Finding out that she was setting him up the whole time, however, that was a lie.. She was leaving him, fed up, couldn't take no more of his abuse, sleeping around with other women and doing drugs. He went crazy, too crazy that is...Putting the poor girl in the hospital for three months and stomping her baby brother out for attempting to question him about his sister. Four months later he gets nabbed by the Authorities. Doing six months in the County Jail before receiving a one million dollar bail. Laying low for the time being,his sister and lawyers orders. Never the less you know he had to have his drugs and bitches around. Lounging in his sister's condominium, drinking, smoking and sexing. Martha didn't care, just as long as he stayed out the Ghettoes for the time being. Believing what ever he told her, he said he didn't do it, and that's all she wanted to hear. Loving him to much made her naive to his life style.

Making her last appearance on the runway after the Mexican supermodels Santana displayed a marvelous red satin Jaquetta Lanee' Farah full length gown with matching sandals, by Negus Farah. Razzle dazzle here comes our supermodel of the year, feast your eyes on this hot momma. Wearing a gold sleeveless beaded fishnet full length gown, worn over a gold sheer satin push up bra and matching lace panties, by Trenae' octavia Farah with gold sandals by Negus Farah. Farah and Vataz are the hottest designers this year, and when it comes to fashion they're at the top of the line. Martha slowly struts in a enticing manner, arousing the crowed of men who were cheering her own. Shouts of encouragement coming from other models who admired her beauty. Inquiring in her dressing room before coming out about the man who gave her those beautiful roses. Mrs. Allred told her who he was and her impulse increased. She knew she had to make a spectacular appearance, that's why she choose this revealing outfit. Wanting badly to get a position in the big Corporate world, and Farah was definitely recognizable through out the Corporate world. Taking her sweet time striding to the end of the runway. Looking directly at Raheem with this devilish smile, and saying to herself.'If i can just get his attention, his full attention,he might ask me out to dinner. He is a single successful man and young...Who cares it's only by four years. I'll do what ever i have to do to scale the corporate ladder. OOO'! HE sooo handsome! Who knows he might be my first, and i know he enjoys watching me. "WOW!"Raheem blurted. "Never has she shown this much of her body in her whole two years of modeling,"Bernard grumbly whispered. " " There's always a first time for everything,"Father utter. Raheem thought to himself.'She's being very seductive staring at me like that....I must say,with that stupendous rump, and curvaceous hips, whencesoever she go.....I'll be there. Steady walking towards him in a alluring manner. He acknowledges those big beautiful dark brown aureoles she possessed. "I'mma sex that,"he whispers while fantasizing on how many ways he could flip that figure.. Stopping in front of him and spinning slowly,so he can get a better look. "Impressing!" he said lustfully. Hearing him clearly,hence kneeling down,and blowing him a kiss before handing him a rose that was given to her by someone else. Rising slowly, and blowing kisses to the rest of them. Father blushes, the security guards saluted her out of respect, and Bernard blows her a big kiss back. Thinking to himself, she's just doing her job, who am i to worry.... she already assured me that i would be her first and last.Damn that ass is fatter than two watermelons. Walking back down the runway, tits jumping and ass wobbling. THinking to herself,'I know i got him, but i can't let him know that and i hope Bernard's not mad at me for being so flirtatious. As Raheem thought to himself. steady watching, fabulous!...I enjoyed myself.....It's time to call Mikasa and give her all this arousing desires inside of me.

"Mama how I look?" Mikasa asked. Wearing a black sheer body suit worn over a black satin push up bra and panties set. "You look pretty darling....so my baby's back to normal, you finally got over him, and mommy's happy for you." what her momma didn't know was that, they were still seeing each other. Sneaking off once a week, just to get their freak on. "Excuse me ma'am." "Yes, what is it Omar?" mikasa asked. Omar was the handsome butler, the one her mother's been sexing for two years. He was from Africa, spoke three different languages and a master of the arts. He was only two years older than her mother, and she was 44. "You have a scheduled appointment to meet with a very dear friend, at Sandals Resort in Jamaica.... Your flight leaves out in an hour," He said gracefully. "OOO!.... so we have a secret admirer," Miss William utters slyly. Paying her mother no mind because she knew exactly who it was. Quickly smooching her, before leaving her presence. "Damn he must be a winner, storming out of here like that," Miss Williams commented surprisingly. "Omar, do me a favor? pour me a drink and come massage my body."Giving her this disturbing gaze. "Alright,Already!" he said in a sensual manner Never wanting her to drink, that's a violation in his eyes. "I, uhhh....hope this isn't inappropriate," she stammered. Consciously rubbing that bulge in his trousers and licking his upper lip. Soon they were caught in an impassioned clinch behind the den door. This was sexual harassment on the job for sure.

Loosening Omar's belt, sliding her hand down the inside of his thigh. "I hope this isn't harassment," she whispered. Not responding to her statement as he lifted her skirt, cupped her satin encased booty and went down to kiss her cute belly button. Despite her immediate head rush. Undauntedly, he tears off her satin panties and lewdly licked her puffy vulva. "Wait, she blurted, lifting his chin to meet her gaze." "I'm your bitch for life." she moans. "You certainly are." She's a 5'10" brunette with nice size boobs and legs up to her ass. Stretching her out on the den floor, positioning her cheeks and slurping on those big nipples. His penis grew to an enormous size, nearly the size of her arm. "Fuck my tight pussy! stick it in deep!" she moans. And doing just that as his manhood wallows in her cum juice, thrusting all 10 inches inside of her. "OHHHH YEAHHH!" he moaned "Oh Yes! it's in my stomach Fuck me! Fuck me! Ride my cunt!" she cried. Opening her womb for harder penetration. Lifting her ankles to her ears and plunging deep inside of her wet box. OHHH-OOOHH-OOOF!" she wailed, expanding herself to accomodate his bulky injection of muscle. "Cum in me please!" "I think I'm ready," he said breathlessly. She already fired off three or four orgasms. Rammig it right, before shooting his hot thick cum. "Unbelievable!" he barked, before collapsing on her tender body. She was ready for some more action packed lustful sex. Rolling him over with his help. Mounting his thick rod while massaging his broad shoulders with her soft palms and long nails. "Give it to me," she moaned.

CHAPTER 7.........THREE WEEKS LATER   JULY 15, 1999

Abording a private jet owned by FARAH ENTERPRISE. "Good day miss jeffries." "Hey! Hubert." "You look lovely as always " " Why thank you." Hubert's their private pilot, working for farah enterprise for some years. "Are you looking forward to your trip to Beijing,China." "Yes sir mr. hubert, I'm looking very forward to my trip," Martha said sensual. Mrs. Allred steady running her mouth, giving her team the third degree. However, that's her job to make sure everythings in order. "510 to radio tower, ready for departure whenever you are." While checking his instruments, he announces to all passengers. "Please buckle up we will be taking off in just a moment." "Radio tower to flight 510." "Yes i hear you," Hubert said. "Please precede to runway 4,5,6, for departure." "Roger Radio tower." "ten four good buddy."

Danny waits for his sister to go on her trip before taking his own. Miami,Florida was his destination,being escorted by four lovely sisters from the hood, Barbra, Sophronia, Ashley and Brenda. "Yall know what we gotta do right?"Danny asked. Everyone said,"Yes!" "You bitches get this right, I'll take good care of you." Danny making a transaction with a Drug lord, purchasing four keys of raw Heroin, ten keys of raw cocain and five semiautomatic weapons. Paying a total of 1.5 Million dollars for everything including all traveling expenses.

"Honey, will you get that for me!"Tiffany yells. Enjoying themselves in one of the expensive Hotels in Beijing,China, awaiting their big day tomorrow. Doing a modeling session for the Chinese Emperor,American, African, Britain, Russian and Japanese Ambassadors as well. "Hey!Martha." "What's up travis, and where's my girl at?" giving her a kiss on the cheek before answering her question. "She's in the shower cleaning that beautiful body of hers." "how's the children?" "The boys are fine." tiffany and travis had a set of twins though travis is a twin himself. "HEYYY GIRL!" Tiffany yells. Screaming at the top of their lungs, they were so happy to see each other. Being away from one another for six months, that's too long for friends who's use to seeing each other everyday. Tears dripping emotions flowing. "I miss you so much,"Tiffany whispers. "Me too girl, and poor Yasha." "She's due anyday now." Yasha's in Jamaica anticipating her first delivery. Mark was so happy, a real man, leaving the street life alone and wanting very much for his bestfriend danny to come back home with him, however he was to for gone.

"Girl put something on, so we can hang out and see the sights." Tiffany gives travis this strange look. "Travis, I hope you don't mind me kidnapping her for a couple of hours." "I know it's been a while go on and enjoy yourselfs," Travis commented. "Thank you honey your so understanding and i love you very much,"Tiffany whispered softly. Before planting herself on his lap and giving him a hot wet kiss. Palming her behind while saying "Don't do nothing i wouldn't do.' He knew she was very flirtatious and easy to persuade, however Martha wasn't that type of person and this made him more relaxed.

"When he comes back from his trip, i want him dead." said kane, with this dreadful expression. Kibbles immediately takes the hit, it was his cousins that was brutally assaulted."Leave him to me," kibbles said scornfully. "Don't fuck this up kid!" " I won't, trust me....If i get caught , just take care of my peoples." " You don't have to say that man, that's mandatory" said killer. "Here's his address, a closed casket, no more -no less."

"Girl this limos beautiful," Tiffany said. "Nothing but the best baby.....Bernard takes good care of me." "Did you let him touch that yet?"v "Hell no!" when he put a ring on this finger, then he gets to smell it, hit it, and if he likes taste it." They laugh joyfully.

The night's young and so are they. Life's been good to them, rising to the top, and who knows what their futures may bring. Tomorrow's never promised however death is and always will be. Struggle is the foundation of success, achievement is the basis for hardwork and strength. Martha loves instant gratification and that's exactly what she's been receiving. Her main goal is to lead a corporation,call the shots, and to make away for the women on this planet. Her saying is: 'A man can only satify her, when need be.' She's like a sven forty-seven aircraft on a runway taking off, however not positive if she's going to have a perfect landing. Money can't buy success, nor can power only the belief in oneself.

Congratulating himself for a safe trip,laid back in his new townhouse. Music blasting, naked women consciously and unconsciously shaking their flesh. Lot's of drugs, booze, sucking and fucking, You name it they were doing it. Five men and twenty women all from the ghettoes of south chicago and danny was the ring master. Stepping out of the bedroom wearing a burgundy suede smokers jacket, with two chicks on his arms. Turning down the music with the remote control before saying "Listen matha'fucka's." Everyone gives him their full attention, coming out of that comatose state they were in. "Yall did a good job, now it's time to flood the ghettoes with dr.danny's medication, the pharmacies are open, and red-rum is the head pharmacist." Red-Rum was sixteen years old, working for danny for some three years after doing two years in a detention center for killing the man who kiled his mother, while prostituting. "Where is red-rum?" asked danny. Brenda points to the bathroom. Danny walks to the bathroom and peeps thru the door. there was red-rum sitting on the toilet with dope on his dick and ashley steady sucking and sniffing. What a surprise to his eyes, not that he was getting his dick sucked but who was doing the sucking. Ashley was a much older broad a thugstress, the hottest thing in town. steal for a meal, kill at will and her nick name was MISS GOOD HEAD. A vampire, profesional flesh sucker and will have your toes curling from severe pleasures. Her body well stacked with that mack truck ass and these 44d's.

Two hours later The Beijing Ballroom was jammed packed with millionaires, billionaires, and trillionaires. Martha and Tiffany were nervous, not knowing what to expect and this is a very judgemental crowd. They choose the best models from all over the world. Selecting the best models   from   the   seven   continents   to   represent   major   fashion industries..........LIGHTS,CAMERA,ACTION!!!!!Coming to the runway first, was our beautiful american supermodel: Martha Jeffries. Our delighted queen was wearing a silk embroidered chinese jacket by Sui Farah. Next Tiffany comes out in a silver plum bandeau top by Farah, with white leather hip-hugger pants by Tahnaya Farah, with matching white sandals by Negus Farah. A loud applause from the crowd. "Girl they liked me." tiffany said excitedly. "Enough talking put these on, yall are up next," said Mrs. Allred. Showing a little more of their bodies as they await their competitors leave the runway. sexually strutting out first was Martha and eyes popping out their heads. Wearing a mettalic mauve silk tube top, with a black silk sheer sheath low slung skirt, black sandals and black soft leather wrist wraps all by Trenae' octavia Farah. Breast swaying, buttocks bouncing and hips wobbling. Arousing the audience as she received standing ovations before reaching the end of the runway along with 4 dozen roses. Smiling from ear to ear with tears aand knowing her beauty was one of a kind. Men were lusting over the sight of her marvelous posture and glow. even the women in the audience were astonished by her figure and that golden complexion. Admiring her to the fullest were fashion designers from all over the world: Ralph Lauren,Vataz Dorn, Calvin Klein, Don Caster, Giorgio Armani, David Cardona, Gap, DKNY, Xavier, Tommy Hilfiger, Vintage Sui, Nordstrom, Lee Yang, and Farah. Not to mention the cosmetic designers: Maybelline, Loreal, Estee' Lauder, oil of olay, Lancome Paris, O.P.I., Covergirl, Clarins Paris, Gucci, and Farah once again having their hands in everything. Spinning so much had her bit dizzy however loving every minute of it,and her heart was pulsating to the sounds of excitement coming from her devotees from Farah Enterprise. Feeling jubilent about herself, as she sashshayed in a loose manner, causing more rapture from the male uncontrollable spectators, and her behind was steady jiggling.

"Daddy, whe're horny," said Barbara vigorously. A brunette with a large ass and some small titts, however a mouth full. Sophronia stared on before massaging that bulge in his black silk boxers. "Come on daddy I can't wait," Sophronia moans while licking her juicy lips. a creamy cocoa complexion, long jet black hair with a tremendous black booty and voluptuous 45d's. Before obliging to their wants, he whispered to red-rum. "You're in charge, keep your eyes opened. I'll be back...I'mma go up here and slay these asses." smaking sophronia on her behind while guiding them to the bedroom. Entering the masterbedroom which had a double queen size custom made canopy bed trimmed in gold, with fine burgundy satin sheets. Walking right up on Sophronia's humungeous ass, rubbing his dick against her tight shiny girdle as he massages her oversized breast. Barbara creeps behind him and slides down his silk boxers. Beastly sucking Sophronia's neck,while Barbra licks his ass and scrotum slowly from behind. Causing an immediate erection, as he slides his prick between Sophronia legs tapping those wet pussy lips. "Barbra go lay down infront of Sophronia,"he whispered intensely. she complied, for she was ready for a stimulating tongue -fuck and Sophronia sure knew how to quiver her insides,sucking that hot orgasmic liquid out of her.Squeezing her butt cheeks, and clinching his manhood before bending over to suck that hot wet dripping cunt of Barbra's. Applying her tonque to that wet pink clitoris,protuberancing it,while massaging Barbra's long thick nipples. "Fucckkk me Daddy,"Sophronia moans. Staring at her vagina before sliding on a French tickler, a special condom with rubber prongs attached to it. Parting her buttcheeks before slipping his penis inside of her. Squealing, from the enormous size of his boner as it reaches the back walls of her vagina. Setting her uterus on fire unlike anything she's ever felt.

Coming back to the runway was our lovely American Supermodels. Wearing a custom made vintage sui white bodice Empire gown, and Tiffany comes out right behind her wearing a vantage sui gold bodice Empire Gown. Both models definitely earning the title Supermodel of the world, and there can only be seven of them. Looking extremely remarkably beautifully lovely,and representing America to the fullest. "Im proud of you girls,"Mrs.Allred said loudly while applauding frantically. Making her last appearance on the runway, Martha walks out wearing a kimono Robe by Sui Farah. Underneath she wore a classic red sheer lace bra with matching lace panties by Jaquetta Farah, and classic red leather sling back shoes by Negus Farah. Strutting sexually down the runway, spinning thrice before stopping, and striking an arousing pose. Handing her a roses was the Chinese Emperor himself. Before passing the roses to her assistance,she blows him a big kiss. Slowly removing the robe, revealing her flat perfect stomach and flaunting those marvelous curves. Her bust stood erect, nipples pointing and her butt muscles were sitting firm. knowing she dominated the runways, when ever she models.The camera men high lighting ever inch of her gorgeous shape, and magnificent features. Moving slowly giving photographers a excellent gaze, while shaking her buttcheeks unconsciously and breast steady bouning. This babe was definitely a site to see and being blessed with such beauty made her headstrong.

Relaxing in his Queensize between Barbra and Sophronia smoking marijuana. "Daddy was it good?"asked Sophronia. "You bitches aint no joke,"he mutters. Smiling with appreciation, as she rubs his cock and sucks on his nipples.. "Are you ready for round two?"Barbra utters mischievously. Over the fence, Making his way towards the balcony.....no one hears him. "You ever got your penis sucked while watching the moon?"Ashely asked mischievously while palming his cock. Ignoring her, and loving every minute of it, getting his rod slobbed by a much older woman left him in a trance. He dreamt about her,when he was a young whippersnapper.. "You're bigger than the average for your age,"she mutters. Reminiscing about the time he walked in on her and his mother, eating,sucking and fucking. As he looked on,they never noticed his presence,however she took good care of herself,never letting the drugs completely take over her existence. Hugging her from behind,so his penis could rub against that plump ass she hauled before cuffing those massive breast. "Lets go,"he said anxiously. Making their way out on the balcony and what he didn't know was that Kibbles stood right beside the sliding screen door. watching, as Ashely pulls his zipper down gently while absorbing ever inch of his manhood in her moist mouth. Kibbles watching, mesmerized by the length of her tonque. "Damn!"he whispers,"How i would hate to kill a tongue like that ." Holding two nine millimetters with silencers fully loaded, waiting patiently for Red-Rum to burst off. "Yeah bitch!..Suck it!"Red-Rum moans. Legs trembling from mere excitement. "Are you ready to explode?"asked ashely. while slurpen and taking in all of his penis, touching the back of her vulva purposely. Gently pressuring his scrotum with her other hand. "Yeahhhhhhh!"he utters. "Are you ready to cum baby?" "Yes,ash." "I want you to cum all in my mouth. Frantically sucking until he shot his load in her mouth and all over her face. At this time, Kibbles makes himself noticable, eyes expanded. "What the hell!"barked Red-Rum. Those were his last words,eight shots to the head and chest area. Ashely jumps up expeditiously,wasting no time before opening the screen door unfortunately he puts six in her back and head. Entering the town house like a mad man shooting everyone and everything in site. Mean while Danny was still sexing Barbra doggystyle, riding that cunt furiously while slapping her buttcheeks. Sophronia incouraging her, "You can take the pain, baby.." Tears in her eyes as she buried her head in the pillow giving her that dope dick, though she pleaded for it. Plunging away as he stared at the pussy juices, gushing simultaneously grunting from severe pain. "Fuck me daddy!"She yells,"Is that all you got!?" Steady pumping ,sweat dripping from his forehead on her back, as it rolls down that marvelous arch she has making her vagina very moist and creamy. " Give it to me!Give it to me!" said Barbra boisterously,"Man you can do better than that!" Sneaking inside Danny's master bed room and no one noticed him. Barbra and Danny were having a hard sex sesion, while Sophronia was at the head of the bed getting her sniff on. There rested a round small size Java table with two ancient oak wood chairs. Thinking to himself, 'this is a real live hardcore xxx porno flick,better then the ones i have at home.' Taking a seat and placing his feet on the table in a cross position, watching strongly and enjoying the sex activities.

Reaching the end of the runway was Martha,spinning erotically with this ethereal body glow and feeling fervor while striding back down the runway. Receiving another standing ovation, and her hips and buttocks conspicuously buxom.

Danny's about to explode. "You're ready to cum aren't you daddy?" Asked Barbra. Riding him back was she, ready to release the hottest orgasm she'd ever had. "CUUMMM INNN MEEE!!!" she moans desirable "YEEAAHHH!" He squeals before before dropping a load inside of her, ramming faster and faster. Ecstacy fills the room as he embraced her waist, slowly stroking. Applauding their works, "Cut....Bravo! Bravo! Fabulous! Fantastic ! Fascinating!...Thumbs up!, however, I'm sorry you won't be able to share this intensifying scene with any producers...Hate to intervene." Kibbles said maliciously. "How the fuck did you get in here?" Danny barked. Reaching underneath the pillows was Sophronia. "Motha'fuckaaa!" she yells before firing Danny's forty-five automatic. diving to the floor, while releasing his whole clip, hitting her five times before falling to her death. Reaching for his next nine, before Danny makes it to his walk in closet, hitting him nine times all over. Still squirming on the floor was Danny, walking over him and putting one in his head before collapsing to his death. Barbra couldn't move, staring at him in a state of shock. she was so beautiful and young however, she seen his face so she had to go. Dropping her head because she knew he would kill her next, jumping to her feet and running straight at him with a razor blade screaming out of fear. Dropping to her face, as he released six shots, stopping her dead in her tracks. Vanishing and leaving no witnesses obliterating the whole town house.

Martha feels what appeared to be a large mass of energy leaving her body."Are you alright honey?" asked Mrs. Allred. "I don't know." "What is it?" "A strong dizzy spell I guess." Knowing something was wrong. "Pass me my cell phone." Immediately calling her brother, and there was no answer. "Martha!, Martha!, Girl we won," Tiffany yelled, jumping and screaming from mere excitement. "We did it girl," Martha cried with tears. Holding one another real tight "I wish Yasha was here," Tiffany said emotionally. "She is girl," said Martha pointing to their hearts. "Would yall get dressed, before they call yall for yall awards....Let's go! Let's go! Let's go!" Mrs. Allred blurted. "Mrs. Allred, do me a favor." "What is it now Martha" she asked. "Call the police and send them to my brother's town house." "for what?" "I got this strange feeling something's wrong." "Girl there's nothing to worry about." "Pleasee." "Alright if you insist." "Thank you mommy." Blushing was Mrs. Allred. Kissing her on the cheek before walking away to get dressed. "Martha!" Mrs. Allred blurted. "Yes." "I'm proud of you....I love you." "I love you too,"Martha whispers. A women's intuition is very strong and being as refined as she was, the slightest horible thing done to a loved one, she'll feel it. "Mrs. Allred what's wrong?"Randy asked. Looking very gloomy, as if she'd just lost her bestfriend. "Who was that on the phone?" he inquires. Releasing a strange feeling as she exhales. "Martha's brother was found dead,twenty minutes ago.....They said a professional killer did it," "Oh No !"Randy barked.

Receiving their first place awards, and cash winnings worth 5 million dollars.Jubilantly with tears they blow kisses thanking their fans emotionally as they receive lots of roses. The people loved them very much, Tiffany had on a Black sleeveless leather turtleneck, a sheath black woven satin and wrinkled metal aluminum foil skirt by Jaquetta Lanee' Farah, with black sandals by negus Farah. Martha was wearing a black leather bandem top and black sheath leather skirt with side slits to her thighs, Two black leather wrist wraps and black leather sandals all by Bantu Farah. Being Escorted by bodyguards as they exit the stage. Entering her dressing room and there stood Mrs. Allred with tears in her eyes. "what's wrong?"asked Martha alertly. Hugging one another real tight, before Mrs. Allred said in a stammered manner. "Some one killed your brother." "Noooo!" She yelled before collapsing. Randy immediately helps Mrs. Allred as they carried her to the sofa. Tiffant storms in Martha's dressing room and Travis was right behind her. Her yells of pain brought lots of attention to her room. "Travis shut the door," Mrs.Allred shouted. " what the hell happen to my sister?"Tiffany raved. "Her brother was murdered."Mrs. allred whispered. Tiffany bursting into tears, shaking her head no and holding her face. Travis immediately embraced her. "They killed my baby."she mutters. Not knowing what she was saying in front of her husband, going into a deep trance. He was her lover before she got married and after her marriage, and sneaking off with him several times just to get their freak on. She told him three days ago, no matter what happens in life,He'll always have the key to her safe and the lock to her heart.

CHAPTER 8: ONE WEEK LATER...

Transporting her brother's body back to their homeland in Jamaica, wanting badly to find his killer, however, the police had no suspects or witnesses. Yesterday will be a day she will never forget, the burial of her brother. As the platinum casket descended into the grave she lowered her head, covering her face with her palms,and her body quaked with emotion. As the last words were spoken a harsh breeze swirls the palm trees penertrating the oppressive humidity. Concluding with a song from recording artist Aretha Franklin, 'A rose is still a rose.' Muffled sobs filled the air. Her grandmother, who had appeared stunned and disbelieving all afternoon, embracing her gratefully and smiled while saying,"he's with our Lord." Tiffany never holding back wept freely throughtout the whole service, and fainted as the casket entered the ground.

Waking up this morning feeling very melancholy about the death of her brother, not wanting to let go, loving him more than life itself. She couldn't bear the thought of friends watching her give expression to the anguish she felt. Telling her Grandmother, that she didn't want to be bothered or disturbed. Laying back in her crush velvet lilac shimmer recliner sofa while watching B.E.T. videos. Doing her best to move on however, listening to songs like,'Always and forever,'by Luther Vandross, and 'Inside of you' by AAron Hall, left her in tears. Two boxes of kleenex wasn't enough to soak up this woman's grief. Walking over to her mirror and looking at herself deeply. Wearing a black sheer sheath satin Gown, with nothing up under it. Opening a bottle of FARAH DRY CHAMPAGNE, it was just there for decoration,not anymore. Her heart was aching, her mind beforged and she befuddle herself. One minute happy the next sad and lonely, not knowing what to expect from her emotions. As she turns up the champagne bottle guzzling without interruption. She starts whispering to herself."What am I doing, I have a life to live and plenty of love to give...Danny I love you so much why you do me like this, I warned you and you didn't listen" dropping to her knees with tears. "Why! Why! Why! she barked. "Baby are you alright in there?" Two minutes of silence before she answers her granmother. "Martha, talk to me." "Yes momma I'm okay....sorry I startled you." "If you need me I'll be in the kitchen fixing dinner." putting her ear to the door before leaving. Still drinking and weeping was Martha. The doorbell rings."Who could this be?" Grandma asked before answering the door. Opening the door slowly."Yes may I help you and I hope you're not a Jehovah Witness." "No I'm not a Jehova Witness for one,and two allow me to introduce myself.... Raheem is my name." "Thee Raheem!" "Yes it's me in the flesh." "I've heard so much about you....excuse my rudeness, come in." "The place looks marvelous." "Why thank you Raheem, however, I'm my own decorator." Grandma thought he came to see her."Have a seat." "I'm sorry about Danny and you have my deepest condolence." "Yes I'm sorry too," she mutters before asking him what he had in the bag. "Some flowers and candy." "For me?" "Yes, you and Martha how is she by the way?" "She hasn't left her bedroom all morning and it's lunch time now, I fear for her." "Can I see her?" "Well, she told me she didn't want to be disturbed, but go on maybe you can talk some sense back into her. She talks about you all the time and she's one of your biggest fans." He blushes on the inside for he was one of her biggest fans. "The last room to the back is hers."How would you like to go shopping and could buy whatever you want, it's on me. My limo's outside, here take this card and go enjoy yourself." She was so excited she didn't know what to say at first, however coming to her senses, as she thanks him. Immediately heading for the door. "Are you sure i can buy whatever I want?" she asked. "I'm positive." The card had a limit and the limit was two hundred thousand dollars. Dialing his limo's number on his cellphone.Buzzing! "Yes, Frah Enterprise." "It's me Billy." "A Raheem are you alright?" "I'm perfect, do me a favor, take the old lady out for a night on the town." "Are you trying to hook me up on another date?" Billy asked. "Yes, you need to get married grandpa before you leave this planet, and yall are about the same age. Trust me she looks crazy young." "You ain't lying." "See I told you, don't come back until tomorrow morning." "Oh I won't, if you insist." "Peace!" "Peace Raheem!" "How do we do ?" Billy said softly. She smiles before saying "Oh fine, Raheem told me you wouldn't mind taking me shopping." "He knows me better than I know myself." "I promise I won't take up to much of your time." "Oh don't worry Miss." "Julianna's the name, and your's !?" "Billy." Both pausing looking into each others eyes, saying to himself. "She's georgeous." Saying to herself. "He's handsome, reminding me of my old man." Being without partners all alone, for some ten years and they could use the company. He definitely fell in love with her glowing beauty not to mention her buxom of a figure. Slowly walking up the steps pondering on what he should say. For he knew the death of a love one can be distressful and miserable. Inspecting the house, always security minded, though entering the bathroom. "Lovely!" he whispers. The curtains covered with Indian Silk curtains, the walls coated with a richly hued design, four large Moroccan Mirrors and a Gold Antique Leopard Paws bathtub. Looking under the sink and to his surprise herbs of all kinds, with sweet smelling fragrance, his favorite: "Aroma Tonic". Turning on the bath water and decorating it with rose petals while pouring four types of herbs. Steam rising from the tub. "Just right," he whispers. Creeping to her bedroom door, not knowing what to expect, however cocksure of himself. Slowly sliding her door open, just enough for a peep. Watching her, as she stands in the mirror glancing at her beautiful self. Acknowledging that she didn't have on any undergarments. "Good Lord," he whispers, "When GOD created you he idn't leave out any elements." Her body was captivating, he couldn't believe his eyes and the arch on that woman's back left him senseless. Her buttocks looked swollen, to good be true and her legs smoothly gorgeous. Martha spins to look at her backside. Now her breast were facing him, biting on his bottom lip and holding his breath. "Wow!" he muttered "I got to get that." Her bust stood at attention with large chocolate aureols and nipples the size of forty-five bullets. She was feeling tipsy and very lightheaded. "Damn this stuff is strong." she utters sobbongly before placing the bottle of champagne on her mantle. Still admiring herself in the mirror."HOOO, that's my jamm, Real love I"m talken 'bout a real love someone to set my heart free." Steadily shaking her ass while listening to the smooth sounds of Mary J. Blige. Dancing like topless dancer, rubbing all over her body in a explicit manner. Sending chills up his spine and lustful thoughts through his mind. She walks towards the sofa, planting her behind firmly and sprawling. Giving him a full gaze at her vagina, as she fans herself. Closing her eyes, enjoying the breeze from the ceiling fan. He enters with slow strides, her silhouette as beautiful as her physical body. Staring before speaking, "So it's real love you're looking for?" he muttered. Never opening her eyes however, heard what was said, never thinking her mind 's playing tricks on her."Yes I want some real love," she moans massaging her vagina while licking her lips. She was very sexually aroused ready to have her cherry bust. He calls out her name softly, "Martha." the vibration of his voice quivered her body sending a mellifluous stimulation. Opening her eyes to her surprise. "Raheem, what are you doing here?" she asked mysteriously, while smiling mischievously though to excited to be mad at him. Never covering herself, just the thought of teasing a complete stranger and showing him herself her really enticed. With out thinking about what she was wearing she stood and greeted him, with a strong hug and kiss. "I'm sorry to hear about your brother," he whispered. Tears bursting, as she holds him real tight. He didn't know whether he should hold her back or what. "Hold me," she cries. He does just that before telling her he found those killers. "Would you really do that for me?" "I'll do anything for you Marha." Looking him straight in his eyes, as she places his palms on her curvaceus bodacious ass. "Raheem, do you want me?" she asked submissively "Am I worthy of such beauty." "I don't know." "Well it's only one way to find out." "It sure is," she whispered......The heat is on and tongues unite, he massages her body without hesitation.

The phone rings: "HELLO!" "Hey baby you sound relaxed." "Who is this,GRANDMA?" "Yes, it's me." "Where are you?" Martha barked. "I'm having fun riding around in Raheem's limo and spending money." "You sound like your really enjoying yourself." "Oh, I am sweetheart and tell Mr. Raheem I said thank you once again." "Hold on......Momma said thank you." "Tell her I said the pleasures all mine." Realizing he could see right through her gown and feeling his eyes all over her body, she deliberatly sits in her thong chair spreading her thighs so he could get a good look at her tight damp pussy. Pointing her index finger at him and directing him to come here, he walks over to her and kneels down between her thighs, wrapping his arms around her petite waist before kissing her vulva.Reaching for the back of his head acting like a vamp and moans of pleasure escapes her mouth. "Baby are you alright?" Grandma asked. "Yes, I got to go." Immediately hanging up the phone, leaving grandma jumbled,however she went on with her shopping spree. He rises before kissing her stomach. "Come," he said softly. Grabbing her hand as he escorts her to the bathroom. She couldn't believe her eyes,the tub was filled with rose petals and fine smelling herbs. "You did this for me?" she asked sexually "Yes I did." "Oh Raheem." Tears slow dripping down her cheeks to her breast staining her satin gown. "Step In,"he whispers. She didn't know it would be appropriate, not wanting him to think less of her,although catching her at a very vulnerable moment in her life, and wanting him very much to take her virginity. Wriggling off her black sheer sheath satin gown, falling off like second skin. Naked infront of a man who she dreamt about four years ago and revealing this voluptuous taut body. Slowly stepping in as he grants her assistance, maneuvering her body before saying. "I have some lavender sachets and loofah sponge in another cabinet." Reaching for the things she asked for, when he turned around,she was out of the tub reaching in another cabinet. Purposely tiptoing to reach the lavender soap, knowing that the water would find it's way between the crack of her tail. Allowing him a full view from behind, of her now wet and aching cunt. Turning around, as she noticed a huge bilge in his trousers. Smiling at him while stepping back in the tub and handing him the items she retrieved, he dips the sponge in the semi-hot tub commencing with a smooth rub upon her shoulders, around her neck and down her spine. Tickling her insides with his gentle touch, her eyes were closed in ecstacy. She wasn't just a figure out of heaven sculpted flesh, she had brains to match. Being vracious when he whispered in her ear.Hence being infatuated with her beauty. After hearing those words seductively seeping from his mouth, she began to entice him with small grunts of passion.

CHAPTER 9

TWO WEEKS LATER: AUGUST 4, 1999

Moving on with her life though never forgetting that romantic evening with her secret lover Raheem.Neither one of them wanted to have a relationship at this time. Raheem wasn't ready to settle down, however, being the oldest out of the two she agreed. Deep down inside ,she wanted him, and her first was supposed to be her last. Bernard called the next morning and proposed to her. She was stunned at first not knowing what to say. After 3 minutes of silence she accepted his hand in marriage and he was enthusiastically astonished. Their engagement party was overwhelmingly crowded and expensively impressive.Their wedding was scheduled for May 10, 2000 nine months later. Purchasing a three million dollar mansion in Ponte Vedra Beach Florida, 12,820- square foot mansion, which sits on 15 acres and features fifteen bedrooms, ten bathrooms, 3 swimming pools, 2 basketball courts and 2 tennis courts. Martha was awarded the opportunity to become senior vice president-corporate communicatins for FARAH Enterprise,and putting her modeling career on hold for the time being, focusing more on her corporate rise. Bernard wasn't the least bit upset, knowing his future wife makes more money then him. She called most of the shots inside the house and outside the house. Being CEO President and owner of Young Beauties Modeling Agency and Magazine, under the publication of FARAH Enterprise. Most of her models were from the ghettoes all over America. Her best friends started designing clothes, Yasha & Tiffany Swimwear, Gowns, Pants, Jackets and Footwear. Signing a four year contract with Young Beauties Modeling Agency and Magazine. Worth twenty million dollars.

These women were smart, keeping the money in the family and sticking together. Yasha, was doing great, happily married and owning three major companies in Kingston, Jamaica. Tiffany on the other hand, business wise successful, however, her marriage was crumbling.She was seen by a magazine reporter from VATAZ Enterprise while on vacation, coming out of a hotel room with Father, a partner and C.O.O. Vice President of FARAH Enterprise and this wasn't a business encounter. Encouraging her deeply were here two best friends Yasha and Martha. Travis filed for a divorce and tried to get custody of the children, however the judge awarded custody of the children to the mother. So now he's suing her for abandonment, adultery and cruel and unusual punishment. "That Bitch Ass Nigger Is Suing Me Now," said Tiffany dialing her cellphone again. "I know he's there, pick up Bitch !" she barked. Her blood was boiling, she couldn't believe that he went as far as suing her. She gave him the house, cars and half of their estate, however he wanted more. "Mrs. Thompson we're here," the limo driver said. "My name is no longer Mrs. Thompson..... it's Tiffany or Miss Walker," she said boisterously. "Sorry Ma'am." "Don't be," exiting the company's limo with this malicious appearence. Greetings from employees, as she enter one of S & S main buildings "Good Morning Tiffany." "Good Morning Rae'." "you look like you had a rough night." "I did, when I found out my ex- husbands suing me." "Say What Girl!" "Look, I don't want to be disturbed unless it's Martha, Yasha, or Father...Okay!" "You got it....would you like some coffee?" "What?" Tiffany blurted. "Now you know I don't drink that stuff." "Got'ya!" They laugh fortissimoly.

"Good Morning Darling," Bernard whispers devotedly, while kissing all over Martha provocatively."Not know baby....stop. I have an important business meeting with the representatives of FARAH Enterprise." "Can you call someone else and tell them to handle that for you?" "I'm afraid not sweetheart." as she sticks her tongue in his mouth "MMM," she moans "Are you trying to get me pregnant?" The room becomes silent. "Bernard , I asked you a question." "NO Baby! I know you want to wait until we're married." "That's my boy, now help mommy get ready." Bernard was having strange feelings about their relationship, however, he didn't want to speculate knowing one of her bestfriends was having an affair with one of the owners of FARAH Enterprise and he remembers how Raheem acted at one of her modeling sessions. Staring at her as she comes out their bathroom.Wearing a jet black instant body shaping bra slip, and definitely wearing it well. "Why are you staring at me like that?" she asked, "what's wrong, it don't look right?" Dropping his head before saying. "It looks good." "You're upset aren't you?" "We don't have time to discuss that, you have a meeting to attend to," Bernard commented before leaving their bedroom. "Well excuse me for asking."

Yasha and Tiffany were having a deep conversation on the phone......"I didn't think Travis would stoop that low, " said Yasha. "Me neither girl." "Well you know what you gotta do." "I know girl you ain't gotta tell me.....Father is already on the job, he's going to take care of this whole ordeal." "You really love him don't you?" "Yes I do girl, he knows how to deal with me." "Girl you said you were going to the top, but I didn't know you were talking about that." "Hold on girl." "You know I don't play that....hold on shit! It might be that bitch ass ex-husband of mines, and I definitely got some words for his stinken ass." As laughs filled the receivers. "Well handle ya business, just call me later and give me the 411, BYE!" "BYE!"

"Bernard zip my back up for me please." Respectfully he zips her sleeveless body suit. Martha loved him so much however, her career was first and he knew that. Slowly she rubs her buttocks against his penis, and wrapping his arms around her and in a loving manner she said. "I love you baby and I promise I'll make all this up to you...After I get what I want, we can have as many children as you like.....Don't start getting jealous on me or of me., I told you before, that will depart us understand?" "Yes baby," he whispered in her ear before cupping her breast and sucking her neck. "You're doing it again Bernard, control yourself." "I'm sorry."

Tiffany was going crazy over the phone: "FUCK YOU TOO ! YOU BITCH ASS NIGGER!" Her eyes were watery and she was very angry. "YOUR MOTHER'S A BITCH TOO, AND SHE CAN KISS MY BIG BLACK ASS. YOU MAKE SURE YOU TELL HER THAT.......AND THIS TOO, GO SUCK A DICK." CLICK! Hanging up with tension traveling through her body. After hearing all that yelling her secretary storms in her office and finds Tiffany in tears with her head on her desk. With concern Rae' said."Don't worry baby everything will be alright." In a stammered manner she whispers "He said when he get's custody of my boys, I will never see them again." "Girl he can't do that the judge won't allow it." "What if he leaves the country." "We'll find my godchildren, don't worry." Holding one another real tight with tears flooding the room.

Making her way to the meeting room, however Mrs. Standford stops her. "Excuse me Martha, Raheem's on line two and he said it's urgent. whispering to herself. "I knew he couldn't stay away from me too long, YESSSS!" she whispers "Good day to you too." "Yes it is a good day." "I miss you." "Cut it out Raheem." Deep down inside she misses him as well, The sound of his voice weakened her knees. "Why are you doing this to me Raheem? You know how I feel about you." "I need to see you." "I need to see you too." "If you get those representatives of mines to agree with our presentation I'll give you a raise and a weekend off, only to spend with me." "How will I get away from my fiance'." "Don't worry about that, I'm going to send him on an important mission." "Raheem, what am I going to do with you?" "Don't worry, you know exactly what to do with me." "I gotta go, I don't want to be late for the meeting." "Yeah you better get going, business first.....Do me a favor." "And what's that?" "Shake that fat ass a little, while your up there presenting our presentation....That's enough to make any man submit." "Is that what you really want?" she asked eageredly "No question, Peace." "BYE! PEACE!" She was in love with this man, although loving Bernard too. She remember what her and Tiffany talked about, Bernard was her good guy, and Raheem was her bad guy. "Martha they're waiting." "Okay thank you." Entering the room, as she slowly shakes her ass enticing all the males representatives. Raheem knew that Bernard was renting that, however he owned that, and being her first fleshful penetrater, that gave him an advantage. That works both ways possessing Raheem as well, he would do anything for her, and she knew this. Being trapped in two worlds and poor Bernard if he only knew the truth.

"Mark Honey would you please pick her up." "Come on babygirl daddy loves you,what's the matter." "she probably needs her diaper changed." "Well change it before you go to work." "Come to mommy poor baby, daddy don't wanna change ya diaper.....Yeah! Yeah! Babygirl we're going to fix him aren't we YESS,YESSS!" They were one happy family, without any complicatons and very GOD fearing. Mark was her husband, bodyguard and agent. Loves everlasting for these two, a perfect cipher always meeting eachother needs and confiding in oneanother when ever times got hard. Trusting their higher power to the fullest, never going against the grain. "Mark would you ever leave me for another woman?" "That will never happen Strawberry." she giggles before saying. "Not even for your other childrens mother?"

"Hell NO!" " Now you know the only reason why I even deal with her is because of your step-sons, my three little boys. Little Yasha has three big brothers to look after her.""Look at her, she's trying to hit you. That's right babygirl get him for not changing your diaper."

Playing with her Bedlington Terrier was Mikasa looking all lovely in her snug fitting Farah jeans, a button up sheer blouse soft grey with a v-neck that tastefully envoke feminie sensuality and grey mull heels by Negus Farah. "Excuse me ma'am you have a guest," said Omar the butler."Who is it?" "The head photographer of Farah Enterprise." "I'll see him out here." she started wondering. What the head photographer of Farah Enterprise want with her. She has her own photographer and fashion designer, and no one informed her of some special photo shots. Maybe her lover Raheem wanted some more sexy shots of her, and just last month she took some nude flick for him. "How do you do Ma'am?" said the messenger."Fine. And yourself, and what's the reason for this encounter? If you don't mind me asking." "Oh, I came to deliver a personal message." "And what's that?" "Do you recall a woman by the name of Martha Jeffries." "Yes that's deceased ex-boyfriend's sister and she has my number, she knows how to get in touch with me." "Stay away from Raheem...he belongs to her. Those are her words." She was stunned, not knowing what to say however, scornful saying to her butler."GET HIM OUT OF HERE!!!!" before running to her bedroom hysterically outraged.

Dialing numbers and doing her best to locate Raheem. Having little luck at all and he was no where to be found. Her heart was aching and her brain was fading feeling very discombobulated. She adulated the foundation he walked on,loving him more than life itself. Curling herself on the bed with tears "Why is he doing this to me," she cried. As she loooked at a whole bottle of sleeping pills before closing her eyes. The phone rings, and she immediately picked up "HELLO!" "What's wrong baby?" "Don't what's wrong me, you filthy bastard." She knew those words would hurt him because he was an illegitimate child. "How dare you talk to me like that Mikasa!" "So you have your little bitch sending messages to me." "What the hell are you talking about?" "You won't see this baby i'm carrying for your trifling ass, trust me." As she slams the receiver, hanging up on poor Raheem. Immediately he buzzes for security. "Yes Raheem!" "Take the helicopter along with SISTER RAHEEMA, to Mikasa's mansion, I think she's about to do something serious to herself." "Do you want us to bring her back?" "Yes BROTHER BOOMBAY, bring her back.....Alive!"......Mikasa locks her bedroom door and swallows half the bottle of sleeping pills. Omar and her mother immediately receives the emergency phone call from Raheem himself. Making their way to her bedroom. "Mikasa!" her mother yells "Open this door now, before I have Omar knock it off it's hinges." Totally ignoring them as she steady pops pills. "Knock the damn door down!" her mother said boisterously. Omar without hesitation completely knocks the door off the hinges, and to their surprise there was Mikasa sprawled on the bed with the bottle of sleeping pills in her hand. Omar immediately does an ancient african technique for pumping poison out of a person, while her mother calls the doctor. "Be careful Omar she's pregnant." "I got this don't worry, just get me some warm water and towels."

"Thank you very much for coming, and I hope yall approve with our new projects." said Martha. "Miss Jeffries we approve, our checks will be transferred to the enterprise account tommorrow." "Yes!" she whispered. "Dial Raheem's private line for me." "Martha he's there pick up." "Hey, Raheem!" Martha giggles "Hey!" "Everything went well, they bought it." "Good job baby, however there's something I need to ask you and I want the truth." "What is it?" "Did you talk to Mikasa about us?" "Now why would I do that?" "You know I would never hurt you in any kind of way." "I just thought I'd ask, nothing personal.....see you next weekend." "I guess so." "Where's my kiss." she plants a big one on him. "I like that." "I'm glad you do, where's mines." "KISSES!" "Thank you Raheem." "You welcome sexy." "I love you." "The feelings are mutual and there's a million dollar bonus for you, PEACE!" "PEACE!"

She was highly obsessed with him and desperately wanting to feel him once more left her more enticed. "Excuse me Martha, your fiance' is on line four." "What the hell do he want? I haven't been gone a hot three hours, Damn!" she whispered in a snarly manner. "What Bernard?" "Excuse me for checking up on you." "I don't need you checking up on me, and I'm not a child darling." "I need to stop this don't I?" "yes you do baby, and why don't you go play some basketball with your friends." "I'll do that sweetheart, so I can stop worrying about you." "That's my baby, you need to miss me sometimes, bye gotta go." "Bye!" whispering to herself. "That man's becoming over protective and possessive, but I love him anyway." Bernerd invites a couple of friends over for a full court game, a hundred dollars a man. Riding around in his car was that so called head photographer for FARAH ENTERPRISE, however there's no head photographer for FARAH ENTERPRISE........

CHAPTER 10

"Here we are Miss Jeffries," the cab driver said. Her weekend was marvelous, candle light dinners, slow dancing and hot romantic night caps. never wanting to leave one anothers presence, however knowing they had other worlds to attend too and richly relationships to maintain. Aware that neither of them was supposed to be there unfortunately they were, and their secret infatuations becoming outrageously out of control. someone had to lead and Raheem does just that because she was to weak and her love for him was too strong. needless to say they were being followed by some mysterious head photographer, possessing the most captivating photos of them. The hotest one was the one on his balcony over looking the Atlantic Ocean. Wearing a hot red sheer gown sleeveless, with vents on both side and hot red high heel pumps, sitting on top of his banister with her thighs spreaded enough for his waist. Between her he stood wearing black satin trousers, no shirt to cover that well built eight pack,broad shoulder and chest. Completly naked underneath her gown, as he wrapped his arms around that petite waist of hers, while slurpping her saliva, and caressing her behind. This was Definitely a heated moment.

Bernard checks the mailbox "BILLS! BILLS! BILLS!, what's this?" There was this yellow envelope, inside rested a letter which read: Your future wife has the hots for someone else and this person you know. I have concrete evidence to prove my accusations. If you want more information call this number, however there's a small fee, and i work alone. (442) 728-8888 code 489, time 9:00 p.m. "I knew that bitch was cheating on me!" he raved. Entering their front door was Martha returning from her so called business trip, feeling very jubilant. "Hey Baby!" she said with this cheerful expression. Slowly planting her lips on his. Turning his head vigorously. "What's wrong with you?" asked Martha alertly. Smirking before saying "So who's the lucky pimp?" "What?" she blurted "Don't what me BITCH!" he barked "Who the hell you calling a bitch?" He immediately wrapped his palms around her neck before slamming her back against the wall. Knocking their engagment pictures to the floor destroying the glass frames around them. Glass shatters everywhere. "Please!.....Bernard STOP," she cried. He slaps her several times before releasing her. Immediately she runs up the stairs kicking their bedroom door open, grabbing her suitcases and personal items. Making his way behind her with this evil look. "Where the fuck you think you're going Bitch," he sneered. While snatching the suitcases. "Leave me alone Mother fucker," she barked. Slapping her to the floor before tossing her clothes around. She curls in the corner in a frightening manner she says"I think we need a break, a few months apart from one another before ruining our engagement ." Bernard started coming to his senses, realizing what he'd just done. With tears in his eyes he helps her to her feet. She hugs him real tight, feeling guilty about what she'd done over the weekend, though never admitting her guilt. "I don't wanna loose you,"he whispered. "You won't baby, I promise, we just need a break." "Are you sure that's all we need?" "I'm positive." Kissing one another desirably. He loved her to much to let her go and he's willing to do anything in his power to keep her.

The judge exits his chambers with both attorneys. "Would the petitioner and respondent rise." Rising with aplomb was Travis. "I am awarding the custody of the children to the mother." Travis family started muttering, while Tiffany's family rejoined in relief. "Order in my court," The judge barked before continuing. "Half of the estate awarded to both parties, and I'm dismissing all lawsuit charges of cruel and unusual punishment,etc!" Dropping his head embarrrassingly. "You two need to stop the nonsense because the only one that will feel the pain are your children: My decision was on behalf of the childrens best interest, however, visitation rights are awarded to the father every weekend.Yall will share the holidays and that will be all." Hugging with joy was Yasha, Tiffany, and Rae'. Travis storms out the court room never looking back, though highly upset with the judges decision.

Entering her room silently. "How is she doc?" asked Raheem "she's perfectly alright and so is the little ones inside of her." "Can I talk to her?" "Most definitely" walking over to her bed with this mischievous smile and in a concerned manner he said. "Hi Baby." Slowly opening her eyes before speaking "I'm sorry Raheem." "Don't worry about that we'll discuss that later. Right now we have to get your health back in order. " Noding her head with tears, reaching for a hug, he gives her one and she holds him real tight before saying."I'm having twins." whispering in her ear softly, "Will you marry me?" Noding and speaking. "Yes!" she answers eagerly with joy in her heart. He knew his proposal would strengthen her, and he was deeply in love with her as well, however Martha was just irresistibly charming.

Abording a flight back to the states was Julianna and Billy, eloping "What do you think the kids will say?" asked Julianna. "I don't know honey....who cares what they think, I love you." "I love you too." "Follow me." Popping Billy upside the head before asking. "Why are you looking at her like that?" "Just testing baby, and thats what I love about you that olde jealousy." Giggles filled the air. "Everyone ,please be seated and buckle up, five minutes till departure.

Sitting on her sofa reminiscing about that wonderful weekend with Raheem. The phone rings. "Who could this be?" slowly answering "Girl!" "Hi Honey! What the hell's going on?" Yasha barked. "Me and Bernard had a fight." "He put his hands on you?" "Not really." "Don't be taking up for that motha'fucka, if he touched you." "It's nothing Yasha, serious." "Don't make me sick Mark on his ass." "Don't utter a word of this to Mark please." "I'm not keeping anything from my husband, if he ask I'mma tell him." "I might call off this engagement." "What girl?" "What are you doing?" "I'm in love with someone else right now." "That damn Raheem and Father got you and Tiffany going crazy." "So are we jealous?" "Of what? I have what I need and want." "You sure do girl, I wish I was happy like you." "Oh, I almost forgot...Tiffany won everything, the dismissal of the lawsuit and custody of our nephews." "I'm so happy for her, by the way where is she?" "Her and Father eloped." "Get out of here!" "Yes girl they 're going to have the wedding when they return." "I'm happy for them." "So am I, now she can settle her ass down." "Is he Jamaican?" "Yes he is." "I wonder how him and Raheem met, because he's American." "You're sexing this man and you don't know anything about him." "I just never asked." "That's because your to busy trying to get something else." "Girl! It be so good, I can't wait!" Laughter fills the receivers: "You're crazy," Yasha guffaw.

"Man you need to get out, ever since you met Martha your life stopped." "Maybe you're right Floyd." "I know I'm right man....if she's cheating on you, you cheat on her that's the game and don't let her have all the fun. I know some women we can freak tonight. Bad as hell and will fuck all night, what do you say?" "I don't know about this man." "You gonna miss some strange good pussy tonight." "Fuck it, what the hell." "That's my boy and be ready motha'fucka', I'mma pick you up at eight." CLICK! Bernard started thinking to himself,should I do this or not...I know she's cheating on me. Shit what goes around comes around and she ain't gonna find out. It ain't like I gotta come home early, she don't live here no more. Let me just call and see what she's doing. He dials her number. "Hold on Yasha this might be my grandma." "Girl you know I ain't with that hold on shit." "Come on girl don't do me like that, I need to talk to you." "Twenty seconds and counting." CLICK! "Hello!" "What's up?" "Is this you Bernard?" "Yes, what you forgot my voice." "Bernard, I don't mean to be rude but Yasha's on the other line and it's important that i speak with her." "Call her back." "No Bernard I'll call you back,BYE!" "I know that woman ain't just hang up on me like that, she's really showing her ass. She's probably talking to that pimp." Slamming his receiver viciously before throwing their last picture together into the wall. "FUCK THAT BITCH!" he barked.

Up high in his private jet plane: "Stop Father! Can't you wait until after we're married." "You're acting like I ain't touch that before." "So you wanna get on some freaky shit now hah?" "Just as long as it's with me and you know the consequences for going outside of my cipher, don't we?" "Yes I do." "No other man can touch you again." "MMM, you ain't gotta worry about that you're all the man I will ever need." As he slides her panties off slowly while fondling with her breast. "YESS DADDY," she moans. Her vagina was soak and wet, throbbing for penetration and that's exactly what he gives her all ten inches. "AHHH!" she cried, and his jet was now in warp speed.

The next morning the phone's ringing off the hook. "I hope this ain't Bernard this time of morning, cause i'mma cuss his ass out." It was 4:10 a.m. tuesday. "HELLO!" "Excuse me ma'am I'm sorry to wake you, however, I"ve been trying to get in touch with a Miss Martha Jeffries" "This is she." "I'm afraid I have some bad news." Immediately jumping out her bed, looking extremely sexy in a burgundy sheer negligee with nothing up under it. Her bust were bouncing,and behind just wobbling as she paces the floor. "Are you still there Miss Jeffries?" "Yes I'm still here." "Do you know a relative by the name of Mrs. Julianna Bari maiden name Julianna Jeffries." "Yes that's my grandma." She knew that something bad happened to her grandma, and those two nightmares tonight brought chills to her spine. "Im afraid she aborded a flight today with a Mr. Billy Bari does that name ring a bell?" "Yes!" "Their plane collided with another leaving no survivors and very little remains." Martha burst into tears, first her brother and now her grandmother, this was definetly too much for her. Breathless as she exhales.The F.B.I. agent was still on the phone talking to her, however she goes into a state of shock. Slowly coming to her senses. "Ma'am are you still with me?" he asked. Three minutes of silence before answering. "Yes I'm still here." "Will you be alright Miss Jeffries?" "Do I have a choice?" "Not really, we need for you to be strong, okay?" "I'mma be strong," she said dryly. "That's my girl, we'll be getting back with you later,Good day." "Yeah Bye." Crawling back in her bed in tears, body trembling and heart aching. Creeping to her bedroom was Bernard. "Martha are you alright?" With tears she spoke, "How did you get in here." "I had keys made remember." "Come hold me." He does just that. "They called the mansion first and I gave them your number." "Why is GOD taking everyone I love away from me?" "I can't answer that baby...I'm still here." "I love you and I'm sorry for the way I've been acting." "Me too." Hugging her real tight. "Come to bed with me," she moans. He didn't have a problem with that, immediately stripping from his head to his feet. As he enters her bed slowly. "Let's make a baby tonight," she whispers. Raheem received the same message she did from the F.B.I. "I better call and check on Martha, knowing she's all alone." Dialing her number, though she was very busy. "Don't answer it," she utters "Let it ring we have a baby to make." Deep down, she knew that was Raheem, however she didn't want to start any confusion. "YESS!BERNARD FUCK ME RIGHT!" At this time she opens her eyes gazing directly at Bernard and for a split second Raheem appeared. She was amazed at herself and holds back on the name calling, never wanting to slip. The phone steady ringing,she pushes it to the floor and knowing deep down inside he would come over if he didn't hear her voice."YESS! BERNARD" she yelled. "Oh Shit!" Raheem said, steady listening. "FUCK ME!" she moans. "He's just here to pass time and you're the best." Raheem heard every word she said and smiles before hanging up. "Who's passing time baby?" Bernard asked. "Pay me no mind I was just talking because it feels so good." Steady pumpimg was Bernard, and she couldn't believe what she just did. Faking orgasms to please her good guy. Bernard becomes mesmerized by the tightness and moistness of her vagina, he couldn't hear a thing. Raheem rolls over and started thinking to himself. She's a wicked one, however, I gotta give it to her, she's good at whatever she do...I know she sees my face. Martha was highly upset with Bernard, and his fifteen minutes. She knew he was with someone else tonight or he's been masterbating all weekend and she doubted that very seriously. She kept her mouth closed and cuddled up beneath him. Thinking about her grandmother, brother, and Raheem. Bernard was fast asleep, very exhausted from his three some four hours ago, needless to say he done his best to please the woman he truly loves more than anything else on this planet. Martha's love for him was seeping away, no man has ever put their hands on her and he was the first. He's very lucky her brother wasn't alive because he would be a dead man by now.

CHAPTER 11

THREE WEEKS LATER

It was a painful memorail service, over three thousand friends and family members came to pay their respects,to the great late MR. AND MRS. BARI. No remains were found, however two beautiful solid platinum caskets trimmed with Diamonds, were designed especially for them by Kaheem Farah. A large mural and statue was made out of rubies by Amina Farah. Raheem's future wife gave a live performance, singing her number one single from her new album...'GOD

IS GOOD',JAZZ MIXED WITH GOSPEL AND A LITTLE RHYTHM AND BLUES. holding notes longer than whitney Houston, and sexier than Tyra Banks. Leaving the stage with the help of her body guards, and looking magnificently beautiful in her white satin maternity gown, by Yasha Farah.

"That was great honey,"said Raheem,granting her a wet kiss. "That was lovely mikasa,"said a family member.. "You are the best girl." "sure is darling." Receiving outstanding compliments from everyone. Martha complimented her as well. "How are you holding up,"Mikasa asked concernly. "I'm doing okay,"Martha said dryly. "If you need anyone to talk too,give me a call...Do you hear me?" "Yes Mikasa baby i heard you ,and when will you be delivering?" "Febuary is the month." "I'm so happy for you." "Thank you!" RAheem acknowledges them together holding a pleasant conversation. "Here comes my future hubby, i'll be seeing you girl""Martha whispers. "Hey baby." "You allright?"Bernard asked. Mikasa sneaks up on her sugar. "excuse me honey,"she grumbled. "What is it love?" "My stomach is hurting, they're beating me up." "Ready to go?" "Yes but i don't want to rush you." "Don't worry about rushing me,they come first understand." "Ron get the limo ready." "Baby i've been craving for some ice cream and chocolate cake all day." "Then it's ice cream and chocolate cake you will get." Holding on to his right arm so tight was she. Raheem catches Martha's eyes before leaving his funeral parlor, and throws her a silent kiss while down infront of Mikasa, listening to her stomach. "Do you hear them?" "Yes,they sound very aggrevated... All that singing you were doing." Soft giggles from Mikasa,as she applied a napkin to his forehead wiping gently. Glancing at Bernard and noticing that he wasn't paying attention, throwing a hot wet kiss back and Raheem catches it. They both shock their heads in adoration, and knowing they were out of control. Only one person saw their every movements, and he was definitely gaining more ammunition. "Hi Bernard." "How are you?" "Fine." "where do i know you from?"he asked eagerly. Martha looks miss thing up and down before asking Bernard."Are you going to introduce us?" He really didn't want to do it... "How easy do we forget, would you like for me to refresh your memory?" He immediately remembers for the sake of his relationship. "Martha i like for you to meet a dear friend of mines, Miss Tina." "How do you do Martha." In a snarly manner she responded,"I'm just fine,and where do you know my fiance' from?" "Oh,he didn't tell you?" Tina was wearing a royal blue body fitting gown, by Vataz and sandals by Tyra Vataz. Looking extremely Tasteful and her measurements was 37d-25-38, height 5'10" 132pounds, curvaceously stunning to ones eye. "No he didn't tell me." "Well i'll let him do that,...see you around Bernard,"Tina spoke enticingly before sashaying out the front entrance of the funeral parlor. "Do you want to explain yourself now or later?"Martha asked maliciously. "Baby she's just an old employee." "well how come i never met her?" "Because i fired her long before you came." "You better not be lying to me Bernard." Lying wasn't the only thing he was doing,he was lusting as well. He remembered those fantastic four hours with her and her twin sister. Trying his best to locate them,unfortunately no luck,and now she found him. Martha was extremely jealous,not knowing if she should believe him or what. Bernard was starting to feel guilty about his tree some. He's been with Martha for three weeks with out any interruptions and working very hard to make a baby,having sex four to five times daily. She was giving him all of her attention and he loved every minute of it. "Bernard i'm ready to go." "Allright baby,i'll be right back, i'mma go get the car." Walking slowly threw the parking lot thinking deeply about Tina... He hits the alarm to his brand new 1999 burgendy mitsubishi 3000Gt 2door. A voice out of no where said,"what took you so long?" AS she pinned her petite waist,and forcefully planting his hands on her tremendous ass."What are you doing,he barked. While nervously watching for any spectators. "You don't want me anymore Bernard?"she asked before gripping his penis. "Not here Tina!" Sticking her tongue down his throat, soon he fell victim to her seduction, and loosing full focus. He pinned her against the car and viciously tears off her panties. Immediately she zipped his zipper down. "Yes give it to me baby!fuck me right here on your car!"Tina moans while raising her right leg,so that he could get a better entery. "Ahhhhh!Yesssss!" Pumping savagely hence holding on to his neck tightly and wrapping her long legs around his waist. They were being watched by some mysterious person,flicking a camera. "Are you cumming baby?"Tina asked?.. "Yess!Yess!"he groaned while thrusting his pole deeply inside of her, and releasing his hot viscid sperm. Pulling out of her and using her panties to wipe his penis. "I gotta go baby,"she whispered. "Hold up Tina." "what?" "your phone number." "Here and don't lose it," "Oh, trust me i won't." Giving him a wet slimy kiss before disappearing. "What the hell's taking him so long?..I know he aint out there talking to that little slut."Martha utters before storming out the funeral parlor. Pulling up just in time. "What the hell took you so long?"she raved. "I dropped the keys and i had to look for them." Just like a man,put them in a tight situation and watch him maneuver his way out. Opening the car door for her,"Honey,why you got on all that cologne?" "It spilled." She knew something was fishy,however never accusing or pointing the finger she leaves well enough alone. "Terrific job and here's your pay." "who are you?"Tina asked. "Lets just say someone who enjoys excitement and confusion." Squealing off in his gray 1999 Acura Nsx. "What a strange pervert."she said while walking towards her pink 1998 BMW 528's. Although counting her earnings of ten thousand dollars, in a jubilant manner she said,"Now mommy's gotta go clean the pussy for my next job."

The next morning Martha enters her office in a delightful manner and to her surprise there rested a dozen of roses with a big yellow envelope, which read... Open me up and you will know the truth. Her first thoughts was of Raheem,shaking her head and blushing. "This man won't take no for an answer."Slowly opening the envelope and storming in her office was her secretary. Fumbling the envelope. "Girl will you knock next time,"Martha raved. "I'm sorry but i need to talk to you." "Can it wait?" "No and who sent you the beautiful flowers?" "My fiance." "Yeah right." "Why you all in my business,"Martha snapped. "Woman you don't have no business,your business is my business and my business is your business." "Okay you're right...Now what do you want?" "I think Bobby's cheating on me." "Well if he is,you need to cheat back." "You got somebody in mind." "Yeah,Roy likes you." "Martha, he's a virgin." "So was you at one time,and if you break his virginity you'll be able to fully control him." "He already acts strange now." "Pussy will change all that." "Yeah girl you're probably right too because Bobby always tell me my shits the bomb." "That can't be true if he's cheating on her,"Martha utters under her breath. "What did you say girl?" "I said go out there and handle your business, and leave mines alone." Laughs from the both of them. at this time someone knocks on Martha's office door. "Come in,"she yelled. "Go day Miss Jeffries i have those papers you requested." "Why thank you Roy." Wearing a white T-shirt, black slacks,red tennis shoes and a red pair of suspenders,looking like Paul Reubens. Martha tries her best to hold back her thoughts and giggles,turning them into small coughs. "Are you all right Miss Jeffries,"Roy asked. "Yes i fine." "Well if you don't need me for anything i'll be going." "You do that Roy." "Bye everybody." "Bye Roy." Martha hits Candy on her hip and gives her this strange look. "Excuse me Roy,"Candy whispers with this shameful expression. "Yes Candy." Roy really had a crush on her he was just to shy to say anything. "Do you really need those goggles, i mean glasses?"Candy asked spitefully. "No i don't, i just like the way they fit." "Would you take them off for me." "Do you really want me too?" "Yes i do Roy." "Okay, their off." "Would you like to go to the movies with me tonight?" Roy started looking around ,he couldn't believe that Candy asked him out on a date. "Did your man dump you ?"he asked sarcastically. Wanting to cuss him out so bad,however holds back. "Yes he did." "A man who dumps a beautiful woman like you,needs to get his brains checked out." Martha face lit up from what he said,saying to herself,"He's not so nutty after all." Candy blushes as she wrapped her right arm around his left. "Bye!Bye!Martha.." "Bye!Bye!baby girl." Roy had this big smile on his face,as they exit Martha's office. "Now lets check what's in this envelope,"she whispers. Reaching for the envelope,hence it was to far underneath her desk. "Shit!"she barked. Going around to the front of her desk, kneeling on all fours and stretching her right arm. Still she couldn't reach the envelope, standing while placing her hands on her curvaceous hips and looking around for an object to use. Having no luck, slowly wiggling her hips and sliding her black satin sleeveless rond neck sheath skirt with vent in the back, to the top of her thighs. Kneeling once more, at this time the vice president of Original Style and Original Men Magazines, knocks softly. Never hearing the knocks. Continuing in her pursuit to retrieve that envelope. "One more inch," she whispers.

Entering on his own acccord. "Damnnn," he blurted She immediately jumps to her feet pulling her skirt down. It was to late for all that he already got a birds eye view. Mesmerized by the plumpness and smooth curves, with those black satin sheer panties that just clinged to her booty. "Tony, what a surprise," she said embarrassingly. "Martha, I swear everyday that goes by you get beautifulier and beautifulier." She blushes before saying."Thank you Tony, your so sweet." Tony gave her, her first million dollar modeling contract with the approval of his father's magazine. Tony was the highest paid male model for five years straight, five years ago, before becoming vice president of his fathers magazine company. Walking toward her slowly in this complexed manner and purposely giving him her back. Softly he rubbed against her, and while nibbling on her ear, he massages her ass with his cannon. Sliding his hands up her thighs. "Please don't do this to me Tony." He was obsessed with her and wanting her so bad however, his wife would kill them if she found out and he didn't want to lose his life or wife. Her body was trembling from mere excitement, closing her eyes and throwing her head back. Sticking his tongue in her mouth before coming to her senses. "You just wanna fuck me don't you," she whispered. "Is that what you call it?" Grabbing his right hand and placing it on her pussy. "It feels good don't it?" "Yes it does Martha." "However you will never find out how it really feels." "Are you sure about that?" "I'm positive Pretty Tony." Walking away from his aura sexually before asking him to leave. "What's your problem?" he asked forcefully. "That ring on your finger and I ain't some wam-bam thank you ma'am bitch...Please leave." "I'll get my day." "You thought you almost had it rightnow, didn't you?" "If I can touch the pussy, I can feel it." "I was just practicing for my love scene in my new motion picture next week and thanks for being an extra... NOW GET THE HELL OUT OF MY OFFICE , BEFORE I CALL SECURITY!!!!" Leaving with this sneaky expression and devilish attitude. Forcefully locking the door behind him, finally receiving the opprtunity to open the yellow envelope. It was a big card and a note with first class round trip ticket to Africa scheduled for next month. She reads the note: I love you very much and I would like to spend one more wekend with you before I tie the knot. It will be a private bachelor party just for me and you. I'm willing to pay you 4 million dollars for some private snap shots of the both of us modeling our new stock of lingerie' for men and women. "Raheem, why are you doing this to me?" she mumbles knowing deep down inside her love for him was strong and never wanting to give up the faith, that one day they will be together. Four million dollars was to much money to pay a model for some snap shots. He promised her that she would never want for anything and knowing he was only marrying Mikasa because she attempted to take her life, while carrying his seeds this made it more tempting.

Bernard had plans of his own, he was definetly doing his best to get intouch with Tina. Dialing her number for the last time...."Excuse me is Tina home?" "Yes, this is she." "How are you?" "I'm okay and you?" "I'm fine but I would like to see you again." "Bernard, right now my schedule is a bit tight." "Please Tina, i just wanna talk." "About what?" "I'll tell you when I see you." "okay meet me in Forest Park in an hour and it will cost you because you're messing with my beauty sleep." "See you there." "Just bring the money, BYE!" "Who was that?" "A dear friend daddy." "And what he wants?" "I don't know," she whispers before saddling herself on top of him, moving slowly in a vertical position. Bernard jumps in his car anxiosly making his way to their private location, starting to have feelings for a call girl, and knowing she's a high priced prostitute, however that didn't hold no weight. His heart was beating rapidly and mind traveling through a maze. While making love to her favorite customer, she remembers to call Mr. Unknown, and let him know she's about to meet this Bernard fellow again. He pays her five to ten thousand dollars for each encouter.

Bernard awaited patiently for Tina's arrival, and here she comes. Sporting this black leather lace up revealing mini skirt with two jean style pockets, a black leather Farah backless tie top and black leather open toe sandals. Looking extremely sexy, tempting and tasty. Creeping up on Bernard, she squeezes his buttocks with both hands firmly. "HEY!" he shouted, "Oh Tina, I didn't know that was you." "Why are we so tense?" "I don't know.... but everytime you're in my presense I get this unusual stimulation." "Does it feel good?" "Yes it does." "Come let's walk through the forest." "That's not a real forest." "I know Bernard but you have to give credit to the designer it looks just like one.' Grabbing his hand before gracefully struttting into the illusionous forest. Dressed in all green was Mr. unknow with his professional mini Konica Double Lens. Tina had a plan of her own, in her mind thoughts of deceptiveness. "Bernard baby, I have something very important to tell you, after you give mommy some of that big chocolate rod you have attached to that well built physique of yours." "Is it bad news?" "That all depends on how you take it," she mutters softly. Coming upon this beautiful man made waterfall, there rested this big rock covered in dry green slime for decoration. Seating herself upon the rock while Bernard was looking at the waterfall. She moans out his name softly getting his attention and parting her slender legs. As she stretches her arms out to embrace him. Wiggling between those thick thighs and placing his arms around her petite waist. Staring in her eyes with this heated passion traveling through his blood, and he was unconsciously in love with her. Rubbing her nose against his as low giggles seeped from her throat. Tongues unite, feelings of ectasy filled the air. "You want me don't you?" aked Tina. "Yes," he grunted. "It's easy access today baby." "What do you mean?" "No panties and bra, just pull the straps." He does just that, releasing the straps on her skirt, rubbing on her tender booty with one hand and massaging her moist spongy pussy with the other. Throwing her head back, as he licks her wet juicy cunt and palming his head like a basketball while he slurps up all her viscid cream. Her vagina muscles were palpitating and blood boiling, mumbling like a new born baby. Making his way to her delicious bust licking viciously. "Slow down daddy, mommy's not going anywhere." Quickly pulling his sweat pants down, forcefully swishing his manhood inside of her."OUCHHH!" she whispers, while holding his waist. "Please Bernard slow down you're hurting me." He payed her no mind, steady thrusting inside of her as his testicles bounced rapidly between the crack of her ass. Biting her bottom lip with this painful expression and absorbing all his manhood. "OOOH daddy give it to me!" Ride my cunt!" Fuck this tight pussy! OHH-OOOF! Uhh, baby cum in me please!" she moans stammerly. Bernard was going wild. "YYEEEEAAAAHHHHHH!" he yells. At this time Mr. Unknown was snapping some beautiful shots, his favorite was the one when she spreaded her thighs as far as they could go, getting a perfect shot of his penis entering the vagina. "Yes," he said mischievously. Submerging underneath his body and whispering slowly that she was pregnant. "SAY WHAT?" Bernard blurted. "I'm pregnant." "By who?" "You daddy.....you're the lucky fellow." He stood in silence shocked however immediately he said. "You can't have that baby!" "Damn if I ain't nigger!" she barked. "It's my first and last." "Tina you are a pros." Cutting his speech before saying with tears. "I'm a professional call girl and I'm quitting to raise my baby." "Listen Tina." "No, you listen.... You wasn't saying all of that shit when you were fucking me raw and i told you to use a condom. Oh no you wanna feel the good pussy, ain't that what you said! Now you don't want to take on your resposibility after ramming and cumming in this good young pussy. Let's see what the judge will say about you getting a seventeen year old pregnant." "What, you're seventeen?" "Oh I know it felt like some older pussy didn't it....Don't forget to tell your bitch tonight that you have a baby having a baby." She immediately gets dressed and storms out the park with tears. Bernard just stood there he couldn't believe himself, however he knew he had to keep this from Martha, the woman he really loves. Dropping his head with this melancholy look and befuddle thoughts. "Good job." Said Mr.Unknown before handing her the envelope with ten thousand dollars. "I like the outfit." "Do you really." "How would you like to spend the rest of the evening with me?" "I charge two hundred dollars an hour." saying to himself," Look at the ass on this young girl and she fucks very well...I wonder if she takes it in the ass?!.." Rubbing her vagina. "Don't do that!..Let me take a shower first.. "Let me feel your breast,"he whispered.. Allowing him to fondle her chest,and knowing she was over 18teen. "I just want a blow job." "Are you sure that's all you want?" "Yes i'm positive." "Pull over in the supermarket's parking lot." Doing just that,as she pulled out his cock."Damn!.. this is a big one."she moaned before sliding her mouth down his shaft,hitting her uvula and gloving it like a hand. "Damn girl,you good,"he mumbles veraciously. Never coming up for air,as she steady slurps his pre-cum while jerking him frantically.

Looking at her watch and thinking to herself..'Twenty more minutes and i'm out of here. I wonder where Raheem is,all of a sudden he's become mr. uncontactable. My stomach is feeling funny,like something's swimming in it. I hope i'm not pregnant and it's only one way to find out, I'll set up an emergency appointment with my obstetrician tomorrow. If i'm pregnant, i will turn down Raheem's trip and offer....i hope he understands. I will not sleep with another man while carrying another's baby. My grandparents and parents would turn in their graves if i did something like that...Bad enough i had sex out of wedlock. Bernard this pussy will be all yours baby and you deserve it. I noticed he's starting to give me space now,he hasn't called me all day...I wonder what he's doing,I hope it's the right thing.Bernard enters a bar and orders a bottle of Finlanda Vodka,opening the vodka and guzzles with out hesitation. The bartender had this weird expression,like if he'd never seen any one do that. Immediately he askes Bernard if he was allright. Bernard payed him no mind before handing him a thousand dollar bill and pointing his index finger in a vertical position although lifting the bottle with his other hand. The bartender reads signals very well and retrieved him another bottle of Finlanda. "keep the change after adding up my bill, but i'm going to be here for awhile,"said bernard depressingly..."I got a young whore pregnant,"he burps,"And i can't even get the woman i love pregnant..Youuu stupid penis,..Whats wrong with you? You don't know young pussy when you're in it...What i have to do, all the thinking around here?" Pointing at his penis and chastising it for his mistake,people were staring at him like he was crazy. A off duty cop walked over to him and asked. "Excuse me sir are you okay?" Bernard slowly turned to face the sound of the voice,he was highly intoxicated from downing the first bottle of vodka. To his surprise it was a lady cop. "Ohh No!"he said fortissimoly while shaking his head in tears. "I don't want to buy no more strange pussy young or old,lady....Excuse me!..while i get back to my sobbing.." Standing in a state of shock, not knowing how to responded to his statement,and she couldn't believe what he just said,however leaving well enough alone. Bernard goes into a deep meditation,picturing himself in the courtroom on the stand and Tina sitting in the D.A.'s section with a big stomach. The D.A. approaches the stand and said,"do you know Miss.Tina?" He look at the Judge and she nodded for him to answer the question. He then looked at the twelve jurors,and they were all women with revengeful expressions. He looked around the court-room,the bailiff and spectators were all women as well. Immediately he sarted babblig to his penis in tears. "You did it,..Look what you got me into...You just wanted to fuck!fuck!fuck!..Now they're going to fuck!fuck!fuck!..Meee!" Beating on his dick and Martha walks in with a large sign saying,'He's fucking guilty, child molester.' The bartender observed him shaking. "Sir!"he yelled. Bernard jumped and looked around. "Give everyone a free round on me especially the women,"he whispered nervously. "Where's the pay phone." "Here sir you can use the bar phone, it's on me." Dailing Tina's number eagerly. "I know that bitch is home,"he barked. Hearing the phone and jumping out the shower with water dripping from her beautiful body. Wrapping her burgendy velour towel around those fluffy delicate tits and that plump bodacious dairy air. "Hello!" "don't hello me,"he said boisterously. "Who am i speaking with?" "Oh, now you don't my fucking voice." "Bernard is that you?" "Yeahhh!" "Having a bad day?" "Yes i'm having a damn bad day!.." "You've been drinking too, haven't you ?" "What do you care?" "so our baby's gonna have a drunken father." "You amaze me little girl." "Don't tell me your old enough to be my father too?" "Don't get sassy with me." "Listen Mr.Bernard L.Hall, are you looking for away out or not?" Pacing while awaiting his answer,as her buttocks wobbling slowly. For a twenty year old she was definitely holding in all departments. He thought back to his little dream of that terrible courtroom scene before answering,"Yes! I'm looking for away out." "Listen and listen carefully meet me at this hotel, the clerk will have your full name and place of business...so if you're planning to kill me...you'll be fucking yourself even more.I want a two million dollar check deposit in my account first thing tomorrow morning. when the check clears i'll have an abortion and all legal documents delivered to your place of business...thats not all,you will come over here and suck my asshole, my pussy and anything else i want for you to suck.Then i get to have kinky sex my way,and if i want to fuck you in the ass,you will let me, understand." "Fuck me in my ass!Girl i ain't never did that before." "Well there's always a first time for everthing...It's your choice,you make the call." Pausing for a few seconds before asking himself. "Is Martha worth all of this,..Yes she is." "I'm waiting ,"she raved. "Yes i'll be over in an hour give me the address....Hear me out!..Don't renege on me, you'll get the money and i will comply with your demands when i get to the hotel. Just have that abortion,when the papers get to me and all is true,i'll throw in a extra million but you have to leave the state." "oh trust me!..I was gonna do that anyway because i don't ever want to see your trifling ass face again Mr.Bernard L Hall!...now hurry and get your ass over here my pussy and dildos, aching for your love." Hanging up forcefully and smiling at the sametime. "He went for it,..stupid mothafucka'!...Now i can go home and take care of my momma and two kids.Orlando Maryland here i come,and for all you bitches who said i wouldn't survive in this game. How does four million in two years away from home sounds..." Laughing at the top of her lungs,and vamoosing out the bar was Bernard.

Entering her house ,and in a exhaustfully manner martha said."Home sweet home." Checking her answering service."Baby give me a call you need to hear this,Yasha love ya'." BEEP! "You aint gotta talk to me no more girl,i just wanted to let you know i'm expecting...Love ya' Tiffany."BEEP! "Ah,baby i had to go out of town on a business trip, you know one of those spare of the moment type things. I tried phoning you at your office but you left already.Don't be mad at me it's for our own benefit, i love you baby!"BEEP! "I love you too and i'm not mad at you,"she whispered. Looking in her livingroom full length mirror and noticing that she's gaining weight. Her behind and breast were getting fatter. "I gotta be pregnant gaining all of this weight and im steady stuffing my face like if i'm eating for two. Watch when Bernard finds out,..he's going to be extremely happy."

CHAPTER 12

Bernard was gone the whole weekend and we all know what he was busy doing. Taking care of that bullshit he got himself into needless to say he didn't realize he was just setting himself up for more heartache and pain.That's what he get for thinking with his bottom head instead of his top.I really feel for the man nevertheless better him than me. This beautiful month of August was passing out of existence slowly but surely and the young ones were preparing themselves for the school year. Ollege campuses, the malls, school buildings, amusement parks and beaches were crowded, people getting their last swims on before they prepare themselves for their hardwork in the millenium. Martha, Yasha, and Tiffany spent the weekend together for the first time in two years. The girls night out, plenty of shopping for expensive outfits, dancing, flirtting, you name it they did it a respectful manner. The only things they didn't do was drink and smoke because everyone was expecting, Yasha's second, Tiffany's third and Martha's first. Happy as ever were the three of them, loving one another so much and having plenty of fun.Three beautiful sisters with enough money to last their next three generations. Once ghetto hotties, turned rich with marvelous bodies and heavenly features, one of God's finest creatures. Enjoying themselves to the fullest, lots of picture taking, posture creating and crowd hesitating to watch the lovely super models, jubilantly relish their night on the town. Riding around in their company's gold stretched Rolls Royces limousine and exploring all the private owned clubs in their circumference. earing the most sexiest outfits ever, drawing enough attention to fill up four football stadiums and two airports, "Wow!" You would have to see it to believe it.

Paying the valet for his services."Thank you very much," said the valet. "You welcome." Opening the door gently and helping Martha to her feet. She stretches her beautiful posture before yawning. "Excuse me," she whispered. The limo driver carried her luggage, rust leather baggage with gold locks by Trenae' Farah. Entering her mini mansion. "Thank you Mr. Ray." "It was no sweat my beauty.' "Stop it Mr. Ray, you're making me blush." And so was he."If I was twenty five years younger, I'd sweep you off your feet." he commented. "If you was twenty years younger Mr. Ray, I would let you." Giving him a friendly soft kiss on his cheek, and Mr. Ray displayed a golden respectful smile. "I better get going, good night martha." "You take care Mr. Ray." "I'll do that, bye!" "Bye-Bye!.. He's so sweet for an older man." Heading to the bathroom and preparing the most relaxing bath water a person could ever relax in, rose buds and sweet smelling herbs. Someone rings the doorbell crazily. "Hold on, one minute!" Storming out the bathroom "Would you lighten up already, I'm moving as fast as I can !" Looking through the pep hole and there was this big envelope in front of her door. Opening her door slowly with alertness, while bending down to pick up the envelope she experiences a sharp pain in her stomach. "Ouch!" she yelled "Oh baby don't get crazy on me, mommy's gonna relax in a minute." Walking slowly back in her mansion before calling security. She wanted to know if he left this envelope infront of her door. The security guard told her yes he did, however some stranger dropped it off and insisted that he get the envelope to her immediately. Tossing the envelope on her kitchen counter before making herself a health food drink to soothe her pains. Saying to herself."It's Raheem again and you can't leave well enough alone, hah! I might as well tell him I can't make the trip, and I refuse to open the envelope because it's going to be so tempting." Staring at the envelope with agaped expression and fogging her mind with impishness thoughts. "No Martha, don't open it," she whispers to herself. "Don't be a naughty girl," a voice said. Picking up the envelope before sashaying to her custom made electrical fire place, dropping the envelope on her Black lions fur carpet and setting her fireplace of a normal temperature. Her phone rings "Who could this be? Shit! I'm to tired to talk, I'll let the answering service do what it does best." Beep! Beep! Beep! Hello! I'M NOT HOME AT THIS TIME SO PLEASE LEAVE A MESSAGE." "Baby, I'll be home tomorrow night." "Bernard!" "Yes baby is that you?" "I'm so tired I didn't want to be disturbed but for you i make incredible exceptions." "Now i know why i love you so much Martha." "So how's the deal coming along?" "Just fine." she heard what appeared to be a females voice. "Who is that Bernard?" "A friend of mines helping me with the closing of my presentation tomorrow." "Why is she giggling like that?" "She was drinking a little bit." "How come I'm the last to know about a woman accompanying you, and in your hotel room this late....You are in your room aren't you?" "Yes I am." Tina was being very provacative, licking all over his face and chest. "Please Tina, I'm trying to talk to my wife." "i know baby but mommy's so horney and wet." Bernard was definetly enjoying himself. "Bernard!" "Yes Martha." "Why you cover the receiver." "Because I'm over here doing my best to prepare our wedding and don't want for you to know." "Oh you sneaky devil, you're going to surprise me aren't you." "it wouldn't be a surprise if you found out.".....At this time Tina pulls his penis out and commenced to sucking it. "Well don't let me intervene your planning go right ahead and i'll se you tommorow, with a surprise of my own." He stutters while saying. "I gott-gotta go,BYE!" "Bye!" Tina had his whole manhood in her mouth. Walking over to her sofa forgetting for a fraction of a second that she had the fireplace on. "It's hot in here, no wonder i left the fireplace on." To lazy to move at this time. "Damn i forgot about my hot bath, and drink." Taking her drink with her to her bathroom removing her garments and stepping into that lukewarm fragrant bath water. Submerging slowly as the suds cover that beautiful sexy body of hers. Rubbing her stomach delicately and thinking about the birth of her first child. Will it be painful or will it be daintly. Thoughts traveling through her mind though being very untutored about what bernard's doing and trying her best to be a stalwart women and wife. They rescheduled their wedding for next month. Just two weeks away. The sweet smelling fragrance and steam from the water puts her fast to sleep. Going into a deep dream visioning herself walking down a dark road pausing momentarily and to her surprise there shined this bright beam of light. It was her grandmother walking towards her. "Grandma," she whispered. "i don't have much time darling to chat with you but the lord ordered me to tell you what i told you before, protect the jewels baby, the jewels." Reaching out to hug her grandmother, however slowly vanishing right before her eyes. Calling out to her grandmother several times with tears. Her dream metamorphasizes to a lovely garden and there rested Raheem on his knees infront of a tombstone. She couldn't quite make out the name however she placed her hands on his shoulders. He rose dilatorily with tears dripping slowly, strongly she embraced him and he said. "I truly love you but this is what will happen if I show it. Please understand why i do the things i do my future exists in you. Give me time to make things right and I promise we will warm one anothers flesh every night when need be." Kissing and holding her real tight , sending a strong hot stimulation through her veins. "I love you Raheem with all my heart and someday I hope we will unite," she whispers. Before waking up in cold bath water with jubilant tears in her eyes, sneezing twice.

Raheem was home alone in his movie room watching his favorite movie....DEEPER THAN MY GRAVE. He rewinds the part where Martha starred in her first romantic love scene with actor Freddy Banks the three time Farah Achievement Award winner. Utering to himself in a sarcastic manner. "Traditons, Traditions, Traditions: will ruin the finest royalties in a person. She plays one snobbish, tough and sexy vixen bank robber with that smooth sexy appeal." Mikasa creeped in their movie room wearing a hot red satin maternity bra slip with vents to her upper thighs, looking extremely dainty and ready for satisfaction. Whispering in his ear in a romantic manner. "Grapes." "You remembered." "How could i forget," said Mikasa implishly while planting herself cheerfully on his lap. "Open wide my comely husband." he does just that as she slowly dropped each grape in his mouth. They had a secret marriage not too many guest and doing their best to keep the media out of their personal life. Rubbing her stomache and bust delicately. "No panties," he said. Before making his way to her already wet vulva. "OOHHH! Did the movie make my baby hot?" Giving her this keen wink as he continues too caress that moist and ready twat. Twitching from mere excitement, parting her thighs wide as she felt the urge to climax while admiring his features and strong physique.

"Why is it still hot in here? I thought I turned off the fireplace," Martha grumbled while making her way to the livingroom. "It's still on, silly me." Trudging towards the fireplace, turning the knob counter clockwise. "There we go." Yawning from exhaustion, and stumbling over that envelope. "I thought i got rid of you.' Her inner spirit tells her to open it and her outter spirit tells her not too, leaving her befuddled. Gazing at that blazing fire agaped, as it calmly goes out. A plausible odyssey grasped her mind...slowly squatting. No message on the front!" A voice from out of no where said,"Protect the jewels." Opening the envelope slowly and there was another envelope attached, which read: This will be very impious to one's eyes repugnantly towards the photographer and odious feeling for someone you truly love. Feast your eyes on this, Enjoy! A tepid chill traverses through her body leaving her taut and thoughtless for a second. A taupe light flashes before her eyes. "My jewels are in danger, I can feel it," she sputtered. Immediately tearing the envelope open and to her surprise, pictures of Bernard." AAAHHHHHHHHHHHHHH!HOW COULD YOU! NO! NO! NO! THIS CAN'T BE HAPPENING TO ME!" Holding herself real tight and rocking on her knees with this dreadful implausible expression. Staggering to her feet, plodding to her bedroom with tears, shaking her head horizontally and vertically.....in so much pain, being hoodwinked and wanting so bad to emasculate the man she loved. Grabbing piece by piece, all his garments, footwear and jewelry. Throwing them on a sheet."BBERNARRRRDDDDD!!!!" she cried while dragging it into the livingroom. Fortissimo cries filled the mansion as she turned on the electrical fireplace to it's highest notch. Tossing piece by piece all of Bernard's possessions in the flames and hating the fact that she was pregnant by a betrayer. Saying to herself. "You will be the last person to know that I'm carrying your baby. I'll lie and say it's someone elses before putting my mouth up to say it's yours, you filthy beast! I knew he was fucking that nasty bitch! How could you? In the parking lot of my grandmothers funeral. You dropped the keys HAH! I'mma drop yo' ass with the quickness. I'm not even going to tell him I got these pictures, I'mma change my locks, phones and business accounts. Ignoring him will hurt more than anything in the world, especially without any explanations." Calling her bestfriends for comfort and healthy advice. Yasha tells her to dismiss his ass and don't worry they will all be the mother and father to her first child. Tiffany told her to go after Raheem now, but have patience like he asked for her to have in her dream. Encouraging her to move on and build from this experience. "We all learn from our mistakes," Tiffany says. Dropping one of her usual quotes: "Most men who have no original cultural background tend to do beastful acts,losing all their morals and respect for others, phychologically rather than physically. Mrs. Allred commented."Thank you momma." "You feel better?" "Sort of." "Remember you have to be strong for your baby and trust me he will regret what he's done to you." Dropping her head in agony however she aggrandized her heart and eschewed her aggression. "I'll see you at work tomorrow," Martha said "That's my girl never let them see you sweat, Bye!" "bye!" Closing her eyes relaxing on her double queen size canopy bed, rubbing her stomache and saying at the same time."Everythings gonna be alright, mommy will survive this ordeal and it's just us two because your father ain't shit! He betrayed us for a nasty hooker."

In his den enjoying his evil works:"I wish I was present when she opened that envelope,HAA! I can just visualize her expressions.....surprised, dumbfounded and spellbound, HAA-HAA-HAA! She ain't seen nothing yet, wait until she receives that sexy hot three days of pure freakiness video by Hardcore Enterprise,HAA-HAA-HAA! How could he let a young slut fuck him in the ass and mouth with a black nine inch rubber dildo!!!Oh, Lord! HAA-HAA-HAA! My stomach's hurting from so much laughter, HAA-HAA-HAA! WOOO! She deserves a extra bonus for this encounter, Haa-haa!"

Opening her eyes and staring at ceiling through her glass dome, restless and frustrated as ever deeply in thought about that trip to Africa with her secret lover. Raheem checks to see if mikasa'a asleep before walking out on their balcony over looking a custom design crystal dome with diamond trimmings and lion sculptures made from a gem sapphire. Missing Martha so much he just had to call her and see how she was doing because she never answered his letters and gifts. knowing he'd be taking a chance by calling her mansion directly at this hour with Bernard living there in all. However he couldn't take her stillness anymore. Whispering to himself. "If that clown picks up, I'll have to hang up." Dialing her number swiftly and the answering service comes on. "Should I leave a message?....Oh what the hell!...Martha this is Raheem." she immediately picks up. "Oh baby, what took you so long?" she cried. "What's the matter?" "I don't know how to tell you, Bernard." "He put his hands on you again?" "Hell No!" "Then what's the tears for." "I love you and only you....But you won't come to me." "Stop the shedding of the tears, I told you what i was doing and why I was doing it. Can't you understand that I love you too, however I have two seeds in the incubator and I have to protect them the best way i can." "I'm not marrying Bernard." "Why?" "I have my reasons and will not discuss them over the phone." "So you don't wan to be alone with me anymore." "I thought about it." "AND!" "And what?" "Now you're snapping on me." "No I'm not and you know I'm going." "Next time, answer those letters." "Aren't we aggressive." Her heart started feeling better and the sound of his voice energized her inner being. "I love you." "That's nice to hear," he whispers. "You don't love me back?" "Listen, you know damn well i love you and you better stop snapping on me.... I took a chance calling you this late 2:30 a.m., not caring if Bernard was there." "Damn, that slipped my mind, you sure did. You miss me that much don't you?" "Do I, that's what I've been trying to tell you." "I'mma need two of your brothers from Africa to guard this beautiful body of yours." "You think he's gonna get crazy?" "Trust me, he most certainly will." "They'll be there first thing tomorrow morning." "Thank you baby." "Your welcome, Oh Mikasa just called for me, gotta go,I love you." "I love you too." "My kiss." "Kisses!" "See you soon." "Bye!" She was so happy to hear that their flames were still burning from both ends. "Hey baby you couldn't sleep?" Mikasa asked sexually."NO." "Come let momma put you to sleep." "I like to see that!" Martha throws a pillow between her legs wanting so bad to feel him between her thighs and in her arms. Raheem was in love with two beautiful women, with striking resemblance and his cultural background permitted him to marry more then one original sister however, Mikasa wasn't ready for that.

CHAPTER 13

IT'S a beautiful morning, the sun's shining very bright,the atmosphere's refining just right and the air creatures are richly gliding through the light. Bernard wanted to surprise Martha this morning, he told her he be home tonight. what he didn't know was that he would be in for a big surprise. The locksmith and body guards from Farah enterprise arrived before the sun rised. bernard pulls in the drive way and stepped out vehemently with a basket of flowers and her favorite chocolate candy. never noticing the two African brothers who approaches him vigorously. One of them said robustly,"You must leave the premises,orders from the young mistress."Bernard was speechless for a second,however, in a fortissimo manner he said,"Your kidding me." "No we're not sir." With this delightful smirk he barked,"Get the hell out my way!" Planting his right hand swiftly on Bernard's chest before saying,"Please don't do this to yourself!..I suggest you get back in your little mitsubishi, before you force me too stuff those keys up your ass, sir." Martha hears the disturbance and peeps out her den window with this mischievous smile. Her credence lead her to believe that he deserve every bit of what happens to him. Bernard pretended like he was leaving needless to say he tried to slug the man, and why did he do that . Boom-Boom-Bam-Boom! With in seconds, slammed face first on the hard concrete. "Now why did you try that!" said the guard viciously,while the other guard phoned the ambulance. Martha stampedes out her front door angry as ever at Bernard. "Why didn't you listen to them?"she raved. Wearing a gray satin boatneck sheath with vents sleeveless skirt with gray strappy satin grosgrain mules and diamond framed sunglass, all by yasha,Tiffany,Trenae' and bantu Farah. This woman was definitely to hot to trot,looking extremely sexy and erotically pleasurable. even her body guards had to restrian their emotions. "Your limo's here maa'm,said one of the guards. "one minutes, i would like to say something to him." standing over his head in a Akimbo way. All he could do was look up her dress with blood leaking from his forehead. However, he still had the opportunity to glance at that fat punnany between her crotch. wearing gray lace g-string panties and her legs were smoothly shining. "Bernard, can you hear me?"she utters. He just shock his head, slowly glaring at him with this odious expression. "I hate you!..and i never want to see you again...take this ring and shove it up your ass." It was a diamond solitaire three stone ring. Most exquisite with a center stone of 3 1/2 carat or more,by Xavier Farah. "Are you through looking at my pussy?" As she stepped over his head."Get one last look at what use to be yours,you low life son of a bitch!.." Squatting on his head. "smells good don't it ,"she sneered maliciously. Helping her to her feet was Mr.Ray. "you don't need to do that darling,lets go,"he commented. she stood angrily before spitting on his head and provocatively wobbling her immense behind,as she strides toward her 1999 gold Benz limo. At the hospital in thee emergency room. "What the hell happened,"asked Floyd. Bernard was in to much pain to respond,receiving eight stitches in the center of his forehead and holding a ice pack on his bottom lip,doing his best to communicate with Floyd. "Martha flipped on me,"he stammers while whispering. "What?" "Martha called off the wedding." "What she did it with, a bat,ha-haa-haaa-haaa!" bernard glared at him,and Floyd felt the negative vibe. "Pardon me...come, the cab's waiting and the meter's steady ticking." martha was definitely a show stoppeer today,being the main attraction at work. Wearing that sexy outfit, revealing those thick long smooth legs and those curvaceous hips attached to that huge ass.Toting plenty of luggage in her trunk and her waist was very petite,luscious to ones hormones. One of the building security guards cought a quick glance of Martha's appearance,as she entered the elevator. "Ta-daa!damnnn!did you see what miss Jeffries had on?"he asked agape. "No,i missed her." "Her breast and buttocks was wobbly and that skirt showed a whole lot of herself,..I'mma give her a visit later on." Pretty Tony over heard the guards conversation and immediately he makes his way to her office. The elevator man was holding his breath and when Martha exit the elevator,he looks to see if anyone was watching before leaning out and granting himself a unduly stare. "Good-googga-la moogas,"he commented. Martha knew exactly what she was doing, attracting all that attention,taking advantage of all male colleagues and employees. "Goodmorning candy." "Martha is that you? Girl what happened?" "I'mma single woman now." 'What about the wedding next month?" "What wedding?!" "Your joking,..Bernard let you wear that out the house?" Bernard didn't allow me to do anything...i do what Martha wants to do." "I hear that!" "How's your relationship with Roy?" "He dumped me for someone else." "I'm sorry to hear that...But you wear to many baggy clothing.come,I'mma show you how to make Roy and the rest of these dog submit." Pretty Tony walks in without knocking. "Martha you have a guest." "Who candy?" "Me!"he blurted. "what do you want?!" Tony closes the door and Martha immediately said."What   are   you   doing?"

I want some privacy." "You're really pushing it." "Martha you know how i feel about." staring her down,slowly licking his lips. She had in idea. "Come here,"she whispered. Tony wanted to fuck her right here however,he knew she wasn't that type of woman. "you wanna taste this don't you?"she asked strongly before seating herself on top of her desk,reaching out to him. Martha was being sneaky as she tapes their whole verbal and lustful encounter. He complimented her to the fullest while rubbing on her thighs,bust and behind. "Damnnnn girl!..All i need is one night and i promise it will be a night you will never forget." "Oh is that so Mr.Handley the third." Moving his hands smoothly up her thighs to her hips,making his way to her tender swollen ass. "what will your wife think of us?" "Fuck her right now!"he barked. "Is that what you want to do to me?" "What i want to do to you is make real love...I haven't done that in a while." "You haven't been sleeping with your wife?" "hell no!..I'm, tired of jumping up and down on the same shit. Her pussy,face and nasty ass attitudwe makes me sick...but you cure a brother's illness." Glancing at her tape recorder and noticing that it was about to run out,quickly she askes him another question. "Tony!" "Yes my love." "Who do you really love, me or your wife?" "You Martha,from the first day i meet you i wanted to divorce my wife...I'm only with her for my families sake. My father and her father own a major distributing company and my kids love me to death." The tapes runs out, however,not wanting him to hear the click sound. Intensely grabbing his head,placing it firmly between her breast while wrapping her legs around his waist tightly. Asking him one last question to satisfy her ego. "If i give you all of me,will you marry me?" Tony was to busy massaging her cunt and knowing exactly what he was doing,totally ignoring her. Shoving the hell out of him before raving, "Get the fuck off of me!..You low lifeless motha'fucka'....You're just like the rest of them." wearing this discombobulated look before saying,"Martha!" "Get the hell out!'she barked "What will make you laugh now,will make you cry later." "There's only one real man that can make me laugh and cry with out me hating him." Candy storms in her office. "Is everything allright Martha,"she asked. "Yes, and full of shit Tony was just leaving,bye!" Tony walks out in a suave manner,up holding his composure. "Candy give me a minute i need to use the restroom." Taking the tape and locking it in her wall safe.

Bernard resting on his sofa,not knowing why Martha did what she did, he was lost and ashamed. His life's been a reck since the day they announced their engagement and one hoo-doo after another. loosing three million dollars and a endless jewel, one with brains,beauty and spirit of joy. Feeling very cheated with out an explanation, saying to himself. "I will stop at nothing to get my baby. even if i have to give up my life...Martha you will not escape my love...please lord help me! I messed up but I'm willing to make up and be a faithful man to the woman of my life." Overwhelmingly he cries for help,in so much pain physically and emotionally. Martha spent twenty thousand dollars on Candy,she has a whole new look and wardrobe. " Thank you very much Martha" "Youwelcome girl and i lookout for those who lookout for themselves, you know what i mean." Giggles from them both. Mr.Ray pulls in the parking lot of a very expensive restuarant and opens the door for them. "Here we are my beauties." Holding out his hand pleasantly and helping them to their feet before shutting the limo door. " Martha." "Yes!" "What should i do if a man comes on to me?"She askes nervously. "Don't be to easy going make him work for it." "work for what?" "A conversation girl, i know you didn't think i was talking about whats between your legs." "What if i like him?" "I'mma tell you what my grandma use to tell me." "And what's that? "Protect the jewels." "Oohh,now i know." They both were looking extremely dainty and we already knew what martha had on however,Candy looked just like a candy something you would suck or lick all night.Wearing a boat neck sleeveless with gold dots a circular cut-outs worn over a glod bandeau top and wide bikini bottom, with glod slip on sandals. Her measurements, 38c-22 , 35,height 5'6', 117pounds. Ahigh yellow brunette with a curvaceous figure definitely modeling meterial however wearing baggy clothes everyday looking like a tom boy!..One would never notices. "I'm sending you to Jamaica this winter." "For what?"Candy asked. "You're worth a million bucks girl,wait til Taffany and Yasha sees you ?" "what about college?" "That won't stop nothing, thats what they have tutors for and i'll personally pay the rest of your tuition." Hugging Martha so tight was she with tears. "Thank you ,thank you,"she said repeatedly. " Don't thank me,you should thank your parents for pro-creating such beauty..Now wipe those eyes,we aint got time to cry.We gonna have some fun and those so called men in your life,especially those who dumped you,look forward to them sniffing yo' ass in the near future,Do you have license?" "Yes,i got it last month." "I'mma buy two BMW's 2000 z3's roasters 2door convertables. what color you like?" "Green ." "Then green it is." "Whats your favorite color Martha?" "What evers available at the time." Entering the restuarant jubilantly with both body guards behind them, watching their rumps, lusting. They couldn't help themselves asses bouncing all over the place,and Martha knew they were back there fighting their emotions,however she didn't care. Being escorted to their chairs before saying, "How are you today Miss.Jeffries." "Fine and you." "I'm making it." Tyrone was the highest paid waiter in the joint. "And who's the lovely lady accompanying you." Candy blushes while deropping her head. "This lovely young lady's name is Candy and she's a very dear friend of mines." "Please to meet you Candy." "The feeling's mutual." "what will yall be sipping?" "A bottle of Farah,"Martha said. "Damn he makes chmpagne too,"Candy utters. "IT aint nothing that man don't make,have or own,as a matter of fact this is his restuarant,"said Martha. "Would yall like thee appetizer to go with the Chmpagne?" Tyrone asked. "Yes we will,"Candy said. Martha stared at her before saying,"You go girl it's about time you came up outta' that shell." At this time Candy noticed all eyes were on them and people were whispering. "Why are they looking at us like that?"Candy asked. "They like what they see baby,let them look." The body guards were standing on post alertly awaiting Bernard's presence for they knew he would return. Candy started observing the glamourous structure of the place,while doing so she glances at the front entrance and noticed a large crowd. she became very hysterical, pointing in the direction of Raheem,though Martha was expecting him. "what the hell's wrong with you?"Martha asked. Her excitement lead her speachless. Business men were jumping to their feet at the sight of his presence,greeting him with honors. Martha looked in the direction of her finger and with this befuddle visage,she immediately displaying a bonny and bashful appearance. Doing her best to appease her emotions. "How do i look girl?"asked Martha. "You look like a million bucks...But don't turn around,he's coming." Candy whispering to herself,"He's one handsome brother with a flamboyant style and a smooth sex appeal...I see why she's crazy over him,who wouldn't be." "Good afternoon young ladies,"he said enticingly, blushing were them both. "Hey baby!"said Martha. "Hi Mr.Raheem!" "How are you Candy?..I must say you look marvelous like my Queen over here." Reaching out for Martha's hand,and granting him her right plalm,kissing with compassion sending a marvel stimulation through her entire body. She wanted to jump all over him and the feeling was mutual. He couldn't wait to get her alone it's been a while since he's touched her body and that splendid spirit inside of her. The waiter brings out thee appetizer and champagne. "Good afternoon uncle,"said Tyrone. "How's it going Tyrone?" "i'm doing like you, striven hard for perfection." "Is God the greatest?' "Yes he is uncle." "When are you going to change that name?" "Just as soon as i finish reading the whole bible,Qur'an and my prayers are up to par." Raheem stuffs a thousand dollar bill in his jacket pocket. "I don't need that uncle, I'm okay." "Take it please." "Well if you insist,"Tyrone said with this appreciative smile. Martha and Candy acknowledges his action,they were well pleased. Candy thought to herself.'For a man who has it all he acts as if he has nothing and that nephew of his looks just as handsome as he does...Why don't he acknowledges me? His uncle just told me i look like Martha so i know he wants me,say something somebody.' She was definitely admiring him ,and he was doing the same,however,not knowing if it was appropriate because she was revealing so much of herself,he holds back. She catches him glimpsing at her body though. Raheem intervenes,for he knew their auras were trying to unite. "Tyrone,why don't you join us for lunch." "I'm on the clock uncle." "Go and get the manager." He does just that,even though he wanted to cater too Candy's every needs and wants. The manager approaches their section morally. "Goodday everyone,and what can i do for you?" "WE would like for this waiter to join us for lunch,"he said dryly. "Our aim is to please all customers." Candy said to herself,'Why is he asking him if he's owns the place?" "I will send another waiter or waitress to your table,"said the manager. "Thank you very much,"Raheem said. "You welcome and thank you also." Tyrone seated himself across from Candy. Raheem immediately straightens that out. "No Tyrone,i want you to sit right next to Candy." Removing himself eagerly for he wanted her just as much as she wanted him. Growing goose bumps from his robust energy,as his silhouette touched hers. Neither one wanted to move to fast,however Tyrone thought to himself,"Look at the body on this woman. I hope she's single and she's definitely wify material. My uncle has good taste when it comes to choosing a sister. Should i touch her hand?..It's right infront of me, nah,she might be testing me to see if i'm impatient. What the hell, I'm tired of being a impassive brother. Slowly he placed his hand on top of hers squeezing softly. Candy jerked. He removes his hand immediaely."I'm sorry if i frightened you" he said. "Oh don't worry about that, my mind was somewhere else but I'm okay and you can place your hand back on mines." He did that in a romantic manner, and paying them no mine was Raheem and Martha they were to busy romanticizing themselves. Raheem sent Mikasa away for the week and Martha got rid of Bernard forever, at least that's what she thought.

"Hello!" "Yes..I need for you to connect me to room 145please." "Hold on sir." The phone buzzed three times before Tina answered it. "Hellooo." "Hello baby." "Who is this?" "How come you don't never remember my voice but you tell me I'm your best lover." "Oh Bernard, I was asleep dreaming about our last encounter." "Would you like another one?" "Bernard baby my flight leaves out in seven hours and If I could remember correctly you're the one who ordered for my disappearence." "Reschedule your flight." "Why?" "Because I want you to come out to my mansion and spend a couple of days with me." "What will your fiancee' say about that,and don't tell me she agreed with the threesome." "No she didn't agree with it so I dumped her for you." "Bernard, why you do that?!" "I love you Tina." Tina had to play it off immediately. "Why you want me to kill our baby if you were gonna do that?" "I don't know I guess I dumbed out. If you don't trust me you can tell the police where you gonna be at." He found out the truth about Tina's pregnancy and age,where she was from,the whole nine yards, she played him for a fool. "Listen, I'll give you half of my fortune, you can marry me and still be a call girl but you have to go by my conditions." Knowing her was a wimp at least that's what she thought, and all on her mind was money. Thinking to herself. "I'll marry him, make excellent love to him this time no more half stepping. Get pregnant forreal, have his child and plan his death taking everything he owns." What she didn't know was that Bernard already planned her death. Bernards mind was traveling at warp speed, he veraciously thought she blakmailed him plus he caught her on the phone early this morning. With who? He didn't know she hung up so fast and when he inquired about her sneaky conversation she told him it was a regular and he wanted to know why she didn't make her appointment. Floyd told him the truth about her she has no twin that she's a high price freak who loves to play games. He also told him that he shouldn't of called her back without checking with him. "Tina why are you so quiet?" "I'm thinking Bernard." "What's there to think about?" "I don't know if I want to marry the man who wants me to kill my first baby." "I tell you what...how many babies you want?" "Two!" "How does three sound?" "Bernard are you sure you wanna marry a call girl who's been alot of men..safe sex though?" "Yes I'm positively sure." "Send for me baby." "A benz limo will be there in an hour." "Hold on, I wanna big rock.....better yet an engagement ring to start." "I got all of that." "You're working kinda fast aren't we? what! you already anticipated my answer would be yes?" "No doubt," he said ominously. "Honey!" "Yes deadly," he whispers "What you call me?" "Teddy,like my sweet teddy bear." "I ain't no bear." "Yes you are, your my little boogie bear." "I want for you to suck my hairy pussy like you did this morning before you left me all alone and wet." "HAA-HAA-HAA! I"ll do better than that,BYE!" "BYE!" Click. Tina's abortion was scheduled tomorrow in her hometown,Bernard spoke with the doctor personally and he assured him that accurate paperwork would be sent to him after the job was done." What job? That fake abortion and I wonder who else is in on this cruel scheme.I'm being played from all sides, none the less that little tramp bitch told my fiancee' about our worthless affair. I'mma win this tournament.Slut you gonna wish you ain't never play Bernard L. Hall for a fool or sucker you freak bitch." He raved maliciously with this devilish expression. He was cocksure about revenging those who injured his physical,mental and spiritual composition. Turning up that bottle of Absolut Mandarin with this omnipotent feeling running through his blood and spirit. Cruel and unsusal punishment was going to be the outcome for poor Tina. Speaking to the limo driver in a uppity manner, rushing to her destruction and feeling very aplomb about her plans of seduction. Waving her hands around like if she was directing traffic. "Don't lay my bags that way!" she sneered."Yes ma'am," said the valet.

Crusing up the Atlantic Ocean in Raheems million dollar yacht made by Jamel Farah. The four of them were enjoying the evening breeze chating and osculating. Candy was glad-somely letting herself go, fondling all over her was Tyrone. Kissing all over her feet, neck,thighs, and mouth arousing her to the fullest. He knew exactly what he was doing, however she knew what he was trying to do too, in spite of her moans of not now. She still allowed him to touch where the sun don't shine. "Baby please respect my wish of not now, and I'm sorry if I aroused you to the point of no return....I'm afraid if I do something with you now, you will become very impious towards me later. Don't get me wrong i want you just as bad as you want me, feel!" Taking his hand and placing it on her heart before sticking it down her bikini bottom. "Do you feel that?" "What is that?" he asked with this smirk. "You know what that is?" and he sure did. "How many times," he asked "Twice." "oh you can get two but I can't get one." "That wasn't my fault,". A gleam of disappointment shined upon his face as he turns his cheek while trying to kiss him. He knew how to play with her emotions already. "Why you turned your face from me Tyrone?" He becomes speechless. "Don't do me like this tyrone." His silence became stronger and starting to feel guilty. Wanting very much to keep him in her present and future, she succumbs to his willingness....slipping off her outfit and releasing the string bikini top before whispering softly. "Tyrone.' He turns around and to his surprise her breast sat at attention. Slowly rising ti meet her beauty as she wrapped her arms around his neck throwing her tongue in his mouth. It's been three years since he's touched a women.She would be in for a big surprise, letting the beast out though she was ready to challenge his inner desires and unique physique. Up on the deck were the secret lovers jubilantly relaxing and planning for their trip to Africa next weekend. "I wonder what they're doing down there ,they're mighty quiet,"Martha utters. "Are we being nosey?" "No I'm not!" "Don't worry about them, if it's meant to be it will happen." "Let me find out you choose her." "I did." "Raheem you shouldn't have done that." "Why?" "What if they don't connect." "Trust me they will, he's a one women man." "I hope he is." "I love you Martha." "Oh, ain't that sweet my baby loves me, and you know what?" "What?" "I love you just as much." frantically slobbing one another down, never letting up for air as she takes his shirt off and he unsnapped her bra. "Raheem...what if they come up here and see us?" "Oh don't worry about that, he's not coming up here until i call for them." "Ain't we a sneaky devil planning something before it happens." "Your acting like you're surprised." "Don't push it." "That's exactly what I"m about to do." "oooooo! aren't we horny." "I should hope so." "MMM!"

Greeting Tina spitefully. "Life's been good to us hasn't it?" Bernsrd asked. "Yes it has love." Lifting her swiftly. "Baby you don't have to carry me but it is romantic." "You will never be carried again by anyone else." "OOHHHBernard, you're so good to me." carrying her up the steps slowly for he was intoxicated." YESSSSSS- Tyrone! fuck me baby! don't stop! it feels so good! do you like it baby?" she asked eagerly. "Damnnnnn right!I like it!" Steady plunging into her moist and hot cunt. "Is this pussy all mines?" "do you want it to be?" "Yessssss, i do!" "Then it's all yours." "Will you marry me?" he stammers while asking the question, releasing his hot load inside of her. "YESSSSSSSSSS," she cried before ovulating a viscid amount of her nature. "Raheem you heard that?" "Baby we don't have time to be listening to them." "You're right I'm sorry....mmmm,ahhhh! yess Raheem!" Things are heating up seduction, fornication, adultery and murder premeditated at that.

Undressing her with this mischievous smile."Baby can we use handcuffs?" Bernard asked. "Who you gonns handcuff?" "You and then you do me." "I turned that ass out didn't I?" "Yes you most certainly did darling and I want for you to drill that dildo right inside of me while i'm handcuffed." "OOO,baby!you're turning me on with your freakishness. Come handcuff me and do what pleases me darling but make sure you drill me something terrible with that dick of yours." "What about the baby?" "Oh trust me it won't feel anything." "I bet it won't," he whispered under his breath. Handcuffing her ankles and wrists to the canopy poles, these were the old shackles they used to capture slaves. "I'll be back," he said doubtfully. "Where are you going?" "I have to get the champagne, ice, whipcream and dildos." "Get going baby don't let me hold you up." Staring at her beautiful body and features not knowing if this was something he really wanted to do. Little voices raved in his head.{KILL THE BITCH!SHE FUCKED YOU BOTH WAYS AT THAT AND WE CAN'T LER HER GET AWAY WITH IT. WHAT IF SHE TAPED HERSELF FUCKING YOU!THEN YOU'RE REALLY FUCKED! AND THAT FACT THAT SHE TOLD YOU SHE'S

CARRY YO' BABY KNOWING DAMN WELL SHE WASN'T AND DESTROYING YOUR SPLENDID ENGAGEMENT WITH A BEAUTIFUL WOMAN!PURPOSELY! MAYBE THIS WILL CHANGE THAT DOUBTFUL THOUGHT. YOUR FIANCEE'S FUCKING SOMEONE RIGHT NOW OUT OF ANGER AN ENMITY TOWARDS YOU FOOL CAUSE OF THAT SLUT BITCH,KILL-KILL-KILL-KILL-KILL!} His face lit up from animosity and his insides started erupting like a volcano. "I'mma exterminate that bitch!" he barked viciously. Slowly walking up the steps each step became harder to climb making to the top and checks to make sure everything s in order. "I wonder what he's doing?" Tina mutters. Her intuition lead her to believe that somethings wrong even though it was to late for all that. she tries to free herself however these were solid iron chains. Entering the oom with this omen expression and noticing his appeerence went from pleasent to horrible."Bernard i have to use the bathroom." she said fearfully. "Oh i bet you do," he whispers to himself.Paying her no attention nonetheless he observed her body language. Clearing his dresser before placing all of his utensils on it in a solemly manner. She watched eagerly and wondered what the hell he was doing looking like a surgeon. she didn't wanna provoke him even though she felt the urge too. Lighting candles and resting over the flames a double size screwdriver twenty four inches long. Heating the metal and wanting it very hot, leaving the screwdriver in the flames before turning towards her."It's a few questions on my mind,"he said. "What are you saying Bernard?" Looking and acting like a weird scentist, he said."There's a few things i must share with you.One, i have a man made license to do abortions. Two, I'm far from being a fool and Three, never underestimate the powers of the kindhearted individual....now! who is behind all of this?" "What are you talking about?" "I must warn you for every lie there's a penalty and it will be severe." she knew he caught on to her schemes and knowing the outcome would be death, immediately planning for her escape."To come to think of it, i had the upmost respect for a conning wench like yourself. Then you betray me with this pregnant shit, knowing damn well that's a lie...Take into consideration that i hate repeating muself so i will ask the questions once and you will spill the beans. That's momma's old saying "son are you ready to spill the beans and tell momma the truth. what a lovely lady may god bless your soul as you rest in the grave and please forgive me for what i'm about to do......are you ready to talk?" "Yes baby!" "Don't call me baby, it's Bernard to you bitch!" Her eyes expanded from the sight of him retrieving that hot long screwdriver. "Some man knew of our first encounter at floyd's mansion." "How is that?" "I don't know," she said with tears in a frightening manner."So you choose to lie,Hah!" walking towards her and giving her a kiss and fondling her vagina making it moist and wet.Licking down her neck to her breast. "What a beautiful thick nipple,"he said "Please Bernard don't do this to me!" Slowly touching her nipple with that hot screwdriver. She yells from the pain,"AAAAAHHHHHH!" "Now are you going to tell me the truth?" he asked before spitting on her nipple. Steam rises from her right tit, leaving scathing burn marks. "Bernard,i'm telling you the truth," she cried."He offered me money to sex you while he took pictures." He had his back turned while heating the screwdriver once more. "So your saying this man took pictures of me fucking you and sent them to my fiancee'?" "He must of, if she found out about us." Thinking to himself. Martha had no pictures she would have showed them to me or threw them at me.This bitch continues to lie to me. Approaching her beastfully. "Bitch! there are no pictures, you told her this morning i caught you on the phone with her and you tried your best to tell me that was a client....LIES-LIES-LIES!" "Bernard!Bernard! I'm not lying," she cried. Parting her pussy lips slowly and plunging the hot screwdriver in her vagina all twentyfour inches of it, twisting insanely and roughly. Steam seeps from her vagina viley and in great pain was she, uncontrollable trembles. He whispered in her ear obnoxiously. "I don't feel anything up there miss, could it be that the baby's invisible? We better notify the world of this..Hey world! This bitch is having an invisible baby...the first ever," he said vehemently."HAA-HAA-HAA-HAA!" While laughing melancholy. Placing a vial on her lips filled with vodka. "Drink it, it will ease the pain." At least that what he thought, however she was hemorrhaging rapidly in a comatose state and in grave pain. It was just a matter of minutes before she takes her last breath. Her eyes were in the back of her head, checking her pulse and noticing that vital signs were becoming weaker and weaker by the minute. "Bitch!Don't croak on me now," he raved. Being so croaked he didn't know he was coming or going. Boiling from anger,he said. "Bitch! Tell me who's behind all of this!" Never answering "Bitch you wanna play dead,okay!" Grabbing the screwdriver off the candles flame and savagely he doused the screwdriver into the vagina and anal, dreadfully causing her to exhale one last time. Blood oozing from her mouth, ears, vagina and asshole. Backing up slowly after Helterskelter left his body.We know how rich people say it"He made me do it." Palmimg his forehead with both hands. "What am I doing?" All he knew was that a dead body was before him, saying"I gotta get rid of the body." His doorbell rings. "Oh my god who could this be?" Immediately he covers the body with his black satin sheets, blowing the candles out and throwing all tools in the trash can."Give me a minute!" he shouted. Washing his hands meticulously and changing his garments. Floyd was becoming very impatient. "Open the door Bernard,I know you're home,fuck all that sobbing man! I got something good for you." Opening the door alertly was Bernard. Barging in was floyd. "Man, put some damn clothes on!" "For what?" Bernard asked. "I got two tickets to the topless show, and it's gonna be some hot bitches there tonight with tits and asses the size of a bulls head." "I got something else to do.""Like what?" "You ain't got no date mothafucka and you're drunk already." Bernard kept glancing up the stairs. "You gotta bitch up there?" Floyd asked before making his way to the kitchen. "Nah!" "Go upstairs and get dressed,you got twenty minutes or i'mma come up there and get ya'."What are you gonna do?" "Make your dumb ass some coffee. Smelling like your uncle after he done drunk up the whole bar and urinating all over himself." Bernard stood listening, like a kid getting chastised "Get going!" Bernard got going too, he definitely didn't want him coming up those steps. Locking the door, jumping in the shower and nervously applying lavender soap to his body.

The moon was glowing, the wolves were silent, highline-highline no crime- no crime. The fullness of the natural satellite of the earth's passing time in romantic reverie, aura's in heat and spirits tranquil when they meet. The stars brightness shines over the gazeboes, waters and skies. Martha stared in Raheem's eyes enticingly. "Why you look at me like that?" he asked "Because I can!" mounting herself on him, while laying back in his double seated recliner. Trailing her fingers down his chest to his stomach and below, discovering his longitudinal which rised at her delicate rub. His name seeped through her mouth, desirable. "Raheem." "Yes love." He was definetly spent from their first sexual climax. Though he would do anything to please her and she knew this. Wearing a lavender satin sheer blouse with nothing accompanying it or underneath it. She sure knew how to get his fire burning and engine revving. With this craving smirk she said. "Baby i would like to know how you became so successful and rich, or were you born with a gold spoon?" "Wouldn't you like to know." "Yes i would." Rubbing her thighs with this susceptible expression before saying. "You're not going to believe me anyway." "Try me!" "I lived in a house next to this beautiful precious jewel. When she came home from her duties, I would watch her enter the front door making her way to her bedroom.I fell in love with this woman...I was only fifteen, being much older than I was she payed me no attention. I would run to my room eagerly looking out my window because our windows were right across from one another. Slowly undressing herself placing both palms on my chin as I anxiously watched. Peeling off her garments stunningly lifting my spirit and increasing my little manhood.""O Raheem, that ain't nice invading someones privacy." "I know,but it payed off....sometimes I thought she knew because she would look directly at me and continue on, like if i wasn't there. I'd never seen her panties and bra off during those times." "What! you seen it later?" "Yes I was granted the opportunity to see her whole body, naked I was her first." "So I wasn't the only virgin you had." "Be easy and listen."She started to feel different about Raheem for she loves no man that lies to her. "Some stupid boy squeezes her ass and she became very emotional." "She didn't have a father or brothers?" "Unfortunetly they weren't around. She smacked the boy and punched her in the nose causing it to bleed. He really thought he got away with that, even though he bragged about it. Two weeks later he got shot in the chest twice he lived, however he was never the same." "Who did it?" "Me!" "What Raheem!" "Go ahead and say it, I'm a fool." Planting her lips on his before saying cheerfully. "You were no fool, you were in love." Still in her mounted position shaking her hips slowly massaging that pole in his satin trousers while throwing her hair back. "I'm not finished yet." "I'm listening," she whispered." I turned myself in hoping she would acknowledge me but she disappears without a trace." "Oh poor baby." "I did three years in prison. The only good thing came from that was I met a African brother who came to the states for a visit. Unfortunetly he got robbed and thrown in jail for a crime he didn't commit. He did two years and went back home, he taught me how to read, write and count. Other brothers tried to pressure him because he was a wealthy prince and his wife's a princess. He stayed on the visiting floor and so did i after i stabbed a so called bully in his neck. Father came to my aid, when the rest of the jail gangsters tried to get me for protecting the African brother never told me he was a member of a royal family,nonetheless a prince. When I came home a plane ticket was awaiting my arrival. He showed me to his family and I thought I was in heaven, but i had a family back at home. Plus Father did another year in jail. I promised i would take care of him because his family wasn't there for him. To make a long story short I was poor straight from the ghettoes of south claimph, chicago illinois."That's where I"m from! I've never seen you around there." "Let me refresh your memory after telling my story. The African brother whom you will be meeting soon gave me five million dollars and strong backing to start my enterprise. I took two letters from Father's name, three from mines and there you have it,FARAH. I stuck my hands in everything legally, first music then clothes after my good african brother witnessed my strong accomplishments he gave me an extra twenty-five million and with in two years FARAH Enterprise accumulated, two hundred and ninety million dollars." "You're twenty-one years old right?" "Yes!" "So i got you by six years." "Are you gonna let me finish my story?" "Oh go ahead baby,I"m so sorry." wiggling her hips on his cock. "What's poking me," she moans sexually. "You're doing it." "Well control it because I'm a little bit jealous about this other virgin, cause I know you didn't lie to me just to keep this pussy, cause i will leave yo' ass alone Mr. married man!" Snatching her close to him as he said. "My address was 1508 Brandon street." Opening her mouth wide before saying. "I lived right next door in 1506 Brandon street." She still didn't catch on yet until he said. "Your room was pink and lavender." "Oh no!" "Yes that was i watching you." with glad somely tears she said. "OOOH BOO-BOO, you use to watch me?" I thought that was a teddy bear in the window that's why i didn't close my curtains ....I use to purposely shake my butt to it." "I know, that's what made me shoot that dude, haa-haa-haa-haa!" Softly pounding him on his chest before saying. "Don't laugh at me." "I'm not laughing at you baby i'm laughing with you." Slowly their tongues unite and rubbing all over her plump juicy behind was he. "You shot somebody over me?" she whispers dryly. "Damn right and i'll do it again." "Are we ready?" "Not really but since you're mounted on it......you might as well ride it." WOO, aren't we frisky."

CHAPTER 14

Seating themselves in the front row of the Topless Bar, watching lusciously the figures before them. Chics intoxicating one's soul and lustful desires. One of the dancers provocatively pumps her vagina in Floyd's face. Very fragile looking,wearing a hot red g-string bikini bottom. Slowly squatting and vibrating her hips in a rhythmical manner. Though his head between her long scarless legs and sniffing the pussy was he, submissively. Wrapping her arms around his neck as she dominately smooched his forehead. "You wanna fuckee," she uttered, while pulling his head towards her vafina, burying his face in her cunt. Sticking out his tongue licking her vulva, staining her g-string. Pulling out a hundred dollar bill as he slowly slides it between her g-string, touching her moist and hot vagina lips. Reading his lips very well as he told her, tonight was their night. Rising in front of him, turning swiftly and vibrating her buttcheeks like an earthquake. The crowd of men applauded her marvelous works, others roared for more of her entertainment. Giving them what they wanted as she struts back on stage, shaking those delicate 38d cups and wobbling that fat ass of hers. Though Bernard was there he couldn't enjoy the show for his mind was deadlocked. Flashes of Tina's face appeared before him stagnating his thoughts and horrifying his heart. Haunting him was she in a pool of blood with her arms streched and hands opened. "Would you like a drink?" asked the bartender. "Yes I'l have a shot of tequilla," said Floyd. "And you sir?" "I'll have the same as he," Bernard said with this contemptuous glare."Comimg right up." "Man what's your problem?" asked Floyd. "I don't have a problem." "Get your mind off Martha, she's gone man...enjoy the show for christ sakes." "Here you go gentlemen."

Downing his drink with this distasteful smirk and obnoxious glare. At this time two beautiful women approach them, one of the women maneuvers herself between Floyd's legs. "Would you like a lap dance?" she said attractively. Looking very buxom, ass all over the place and her headlights were definetely on high beams. He wasn't about to turn her down, and saying to himself."I would love to stick my penis between her voluptuous bosom and burst off on those thickly lips of hers. That pussy's probably tight as hell, it's only one way to find out." whispering in her ear before massaging her thighs,"How much?" "Ten thousand." "How about twenty for forty eight hours?" "That's t.v. time." "Check or cash?" "This ass only wants cash." "What's up with your girlfriend?" "I don't know you have to ask her." The bartender asked,"Would you care for some drinks?" "Yes...and get the ladies whatever they want." "What's your name?" "Floyd." "Well Floyd,this lap dance is on the house," she spouted shaking her buttocks pretentiously. This hussy would stop at nothing, grabbing his penis right threw his trousers. Bernard impulsively pulled her between his legs, firmly gripping that ample backbone, caressing and caretaking to her physical properties. She was enjoying his every touch,"I want to go home with you tonight handsome," she repeated laughing. His diabolical thoughts lead him to do things he just wouldn't do, liking tasting her tongue. She loved his aggressiveness as his tongue invaded her mouth causing her vagina to tingle. Her eyes revealed the wildfire to her soul and he knew of her plans of seduction. Pinching her bodacious booty,"Ouch!" she blurted "What's wrong?" he asked. "Nothing really." "What's your price?" "Whatever you can afford handsome." "Is ten thousand good?" "Yes, and what shall I call you?" "Bernard." "Would you like a free lap dance?" "Am i worthy of one.... Moanna?" "Without a doubt," she whispers before turning around and bending over granting him a splendid sight of her inner thighs along with that bodacious ass.

Most of the dancers were porno stars at one time or another and tickets are one thousand dollars just to enter the place, eachdrink is ten dollars. You had to be a high roller to come in in this spot, well secured and no hooey what so ever. Swaying her breast infront of him showing her birthmark along side of her right nipple and incessantly cupping her bust kissing them together. "That's how i like it Martha," said Bernard dryly. You just about give them any name you like, very rarely one of them would tell you their real name unless you were someone special or a regular fan, who just followed them around the world. Forgetting that he had a dead body at home he succumbs to her luring passion and suggested that they leave now. She didn't hesistate to his suggestion, thinking to herself. If there's ten thousand, there's more and once he get a taste of my sexual desires, he would pour out his account to me. She has the qualities, being the youngest porno queen ever to win best female porno of the year award back to back. When horny she chooses her prey and she won't charge him, if he out do her. That's why she told Bernard whatever he can afford, he's her choosen penertrator."Where sre you going man?" asked Floyd. "I'm going to handle my business, and shouldn't you be doing the same? She's ready and hot!" "It's about time you took your head out ya' ass, I'm happy for you! if you need some help don't be afraid to call." "Don't worry I got this, you better control that," he said with this devilish expression. Floyd's friend was drinking up a storm,"Damn girl you sure drink alot! I hope you fuck as much as you drink....""Oh don't worry about that, just make sure you can stick'er and lick'er as much as you bick'er." "OOOOOO ain't we a snobbish wench."

Wednesday evening was a magnificent evening and everyone's preparing for the Enterprises Birthday Bash.........Famous people from all over the world will be attending this extravaganza.Dress to impress and wear your most finest gems. This astronomical event will be held at their Mussel shaped dining room,constructor Ronnie Farah. The place was jammed packed and people were steady pouring in, unexpectedly they had to open the fourth wing to the place. Live entertainment by star singers: Aretha franklin, Monica, Tamia, Erykah Badu, Brian Mcknight, Maxwell, Usher, and Gerald Levert. Groups like......Xscape, Destiny's child, Next, Boyz to Men, SWV, Druhill and The Temptations. Rap artist: LL Cool J, Jay-Z, Master P(No Limit) and Da Brat. The FARAH Achievement Award was distributed to Master P and famous model Tyra Banks. This event lasted twelve hours with the exception of the after party. A standing ovation for the brother Raheem as he takes the stage to receive a surprising award from friends, family members and colleagues. Giving a brief speech of appreciation with unexpected twin tears rolling down his cheeks. Being escorted by his wife, sister, and his chaperone Martha Jeffries. "Thank you very much," he stammers repeatedly before leaving the stage.

Bernard enters the auditorium with two topless dancers and I must say they were definetly car stoppers, looking extremely tasteful, capturing the attention of all male guest married and single. Wearing twin purple revealing jersey gowns with lace insets, and bodies outrageously provoking. He sure knew what to bring to rouse emotions and floyd was no different, though he had four topless dancers accompanying him wearing colorful revealing outfits as well. Bernard was decked out in his tailor made two piece Vataz suit. Wearing a diamond ascot, a white silk shirt, black slacks, a purple blazer and a pair of black Stacey Adams and on his left wrist rested a very expensive handcrafted Switzerland Clerc watch with 5 1/2 diamonds and sapphires. On his right wrist he wore a 6 1/2 carat bracelet and pinky ring solitaire 4 stone rings most exquisite with stones of 1 1/2 carat or more. Martha noticed his grand stand of a entry and it appeared to her like he was really enjoying their engagement call off. Looking extremely stunning herself, wearing a burgundy sheath revealing jersey strapless dress with lace insets, and vents. With stone earrings 1 1/2 carat, a matching necklace 3 1/2 carat, bracelet 4 1/2 carats, watch 2 1/2 carat and diamond solitaire three stone ring most refined with a center stone of 4 1/2 carat. Paying nothing for her fine jewelry it was a gift from her first and secret lover. Candy accompanied her even though her fiancee' Taheem couldn't make the event, away on a very important business trip for his uncle Raheem. Being appointed by his uncle head supervisor of all Farah Restaurants. This was a big job for the young man because there are twenty-five Farah restaurants however he accepted the position and was most pleased with his uncles choice.

Yasha and Tiffany sneaks up on Martha,"hey girl!" tiffany blurted. "Uh-huh I seen y'all coming,"Martha guffaw "Is this the lovely Candy?" Yasha asked orderly. "Yes this is." Candy blushes with respect. "I love the outfit Candy," Tiffany commented. "She's definetly a crowd pleaser," Yasha said while observing her posture and features. "I hope you don't mine me but it's my job Candy to look over our project," she uttered. Candy was so nervous to be around such great beauty and the three of them sparked the atmosphere with their figures and garments. "Relax darling, don't be so tense, "Yasha whispers. "You fit in just fine.....don't she girls?" "Oh yess indeed," Tiffany responded dryly. "Girl loosen up, I done told you that twenty times already," Martha commented. "Don't look, but here comes Bernard with these things attached to his arms," Yasha raved. She wasn't lying he was walking directly towards Martha. "Girl if he say something slick i'mma cut his punk ass,"Tiffany said boisterously. "Tiffany would you calm down," Yasha whispered seriously. "I can't stand his ass, strutting over here like he's somebody......i'mma tell father to eighty-six his ass,"she babbled. "Now tiffany, you know if that happens he's gonna run to Vataz Enterprise," Martha raved. "So what! we don't need him anymore." "She has a point Martha." "I know she does Yasha, but he will only blame me." "She's right about that too Tiffany." "Girl enough of all that back and forth shit!...do you still have feelings for the motha'fucker?" Tiffany utters angrily. "NO!" "Okay then, he's gone plain and simple! I'm firing his ass." "You go girl!" Yasha guffaws. Candy had no idea of what was going on, they all started laughing so she follows suit. "Girl pay us no mind we're trippin, but that damn Bernard we're serious about his trifling ass, " Tiffany mutters."Good evening," said Bernard spitefully before winking at Martha and impassively walking pass her licking his tongue out impiously while palming firmly the booty of the topless dancer closest to her and she definetly had a humongeous ass. Neither one of them spoke back, he didn't care he just wanted to get her blood boiling knowing she's the jealous type. Tiffany wanted badly to intercede however Yasha stopped her though Martha paid him no mind. She's highly upset wanting very much to give him a verbal chastisement. Tiffany's a curmudgeon individual when it comes to protecting her two best friends.Martha thought to herself. How dare he prance by me like he's almighty god with two dirty ass demons staring all in my face. He's really pushing his luck and he just don't know how bad i wanna embarras his dirty ass. "Girl what are you thinking about?" asked Tiffany. "I just realized what that nigger tried to do." "And what's that?" "Get rid of Yasha and candy for me, we got work to do." "Are you thinking what i'm thinking?" "That all depends on what it is you're thinking." "Dismissing Bernards ass now in front of his little sluts." "Exactly!" Martha responded connivingly. Tiffany whispers to Yasha in a persuading manner."Yasha darling why don't you take Candy on a business tour." Knowing that's Yasha's favorite thing, talking their clients to death. "Would you enjoy that Candy?" Yasha asked. "Oh yes Mrs.Yasha." "Girl please call me Yasha, Mrs makes me feel old." Candy didn't know what she was in for and her ears wil hit the ground more then once. Tiffany and Martha had plans of their own,strutting towards Bernard's table. "Excuse me Mr.Hall may i have a word with you?" Martha asked solemnly. "Yes you may." "Alone!" "Whatever you say won't distract my guest, will it?" "I don't know,,,that all depends on you."Waving his hand for a waiter. "Yes, what is it sir?" said the waiter."Can you bring me and my dolls a bottle of Farah." "Will it be dry?" "Yes make that dry." Tiffany whispers in Martha's ear, "Let his ass have it girl." "Bernard I need to talk with you." "Can't you see i'm busy over here and you know my business hours." He totally ignored the fact that she was his boss now. He was acting very impious giving her his back although fortissimo laughs escaped his throat while fondling with his guests.Martha couldn't take no more, yanking his shoulder and pointing her index finger directly at his nose."YOU BITCH ASS NIGGER,PACK YO' SHIT MONDAY MORNING....YOU"RE FIRED!!!!!!" "WHAT!?" he barked before standing."Go ahead motha'fucka make our day," Tiffany raved ominously pulling her switchblade from her purse. He had this gawk expression as he meticulously seated himself without hestation. The waiter approached the table with both bottles of Farah champagne."Will that be all sir?" he said joyfully."Ah...waiter do me a favor? bring the harlots and mr. loser another bottle of champagne on me." "Yes Miss Jeffries." Bernard was highly upset though out numbered so he leaves well enough alone.

The after party was lovely, overwhelmingly crowded and overly influxed. Live music and entertainment from young amateur singers, with the help from professional bands. Raheem creeps behind martha as she stood by the balcony with tiffany laughing about what they just did to Bernard. "Who loves you?" he whispered in her ear veraciously. She knew from the voice who he was, sending a warm stimulation threw her blood while wrapping his arms around her petite waist. Tiffany said pleasantly "I'll be leaving you too love birds alone, love y'allbye!"before strongly granting them a kiss and sashaying across the ballroom floor. "Where's the misses?" Martha asked while rubbing his hands and massaging his penis with her bodacious rump. "She was feeling a little under the weather so i sent her home immediately," he whispered informally while sticking his tongue in her ear, blowing hot wind provacatively simultaneously arousing her desire. She adored this man very much and loving every minute of his time drew her closer to his heart. She thought to herself:he's so adorable I should have pressured him into a relationship after letting him satiate my unbroken cherry. A slow jam came on, his favorite, "A rose is still a rose," by aretha franklin. "Can i have this dance?" he asked romantically."You can have anything I got," she responded lusciously,slowly walking towards the middle of the floor the both of them amusingly and glaring at them was Bernard chapfallenly. Incessantly wrapping one another tightly leaving no air pockets between them, staring in her eyes was he. Mikasa already knew the truth about htem because Raheem had a long emotional conversation with her. She accepted the fact that he loved her very much, recognizing that his way of life permitted him to have up to four wives though she's the first. "I love you," she moans softly. "I know." he said merrily as they osculated with heated passions. Yasha was very garrulous, leaving Candy very spent and her ears were ringing like crazy even though she's enjoying herself."Wanna another drink girl?" Yasha asked. "No thank you! I'm tipsy enough...if my man was here i don't think he would appreciate me drinking so much." Misfortune struck Bernard one again seeing his love willingly embraced in another man's arms cheerfully bodies touching and mouths tasting. Moping to the restroom, as he enters the last recepticle opening a hundred dollar bill filled with cocain sniffing intensively. Bernard was now retrogressing loosing his state of well being and vile vision haunted him. Hiding his inner feelings as he carousely staggers to his table. "are you okay daddy?" asked one of his guest. Cocaine all over his nose and immediately wiping was she. "What are you doing bitch?"he barked. "Cleaning the residue off your nose stupid." "Oh shit!...you think someone seen it?" "I have no idea." "Y'all want something else to drink?" "Yeah why not but you've had enough Mr.Bernard" she said enticingly while the other harlot massages his penis. "How this feel daddy?" she said desirously.

Father and Tiffany were out on the balcony submerged under his arms was she with her back turned. He was massaging her breast and unnoticing pokes from his manhood on her immense buttcheeks."Baby i have something to tell you,"she repeated dryly."Are you trying to mess with my concentration my dear?" "We need to save this for the bedroom...stop poking me in my asshole! you're wetting my Tiffany's secret." "Oh i forgot you're pregnant." "How could you, you stay up in me." "Is that what you had to tell me?" "No!" "Let's hear it." "Boo-boo stop that!"she whispered shrewdly. Though he paid her no mind,"Now if i remove my panties you're gonna have a fit around here aren't we?" "Allright, allright" "I knew that would stop yo' ass." "I love you though." "I love you too...now listen." "ears are open." "We fired Bernard L. Hall." "When did y'all do that?" "about an hour ago." "I don't know what Raheems gonna say about that." "That's how come i want for you to tell him,"she moans before facing him and sticking her tongue in his mouth, sucking all of his saliva.

"Raheem honey." "Yes Martha." "I have something to tell you." "And what's that?" "Oh boy, how am i going to do this?" "Do what?" "Tell you i fired Bernard L. Hall." "Thee Bernard L. Hall?" "Yes darling," she cried before submerging in his arms. taking a deep breath before saying out loud,"Why!" "Baby please don't be angry with me." "I'm not, but why?" Twin tears rolled down those healthy cheeks and Raheem couldn't stand to see her cry. "Is he messing with you?" "Yes." "Business comes first baby never forget that..lift ya' head up and be firm with your decisions because the only one that has to live with them is you understand?" Shaking her head in agreement, he wiped her tears and said "Don't worry you did what you thought was best,and i'm here to cover all your mistakes." People were enjoying themselves to the fullest, no hooey, buxom women and comely men dancing, drinking, and chit-chatting. No business all pleasure however, if a deal comes by billionaires was signing it, and advertisements drew lots of attention. Valets making lots of money, waiters and waitresses wallets bearly folding. Farah catering service did a wonderful job displaying their fine styles of appetizers and decorating desserts. Three hundred and fifty thousand dollars was the cost for such delicious meals and drinks. One had to be well pleased to attend such authentic glamourous gleams that surrounded the mussel shaped ballroom, a flourishing fountain made from diamonds and nine crystal bobcats trimmed in platinum. Murals of important historical original figure heads and leaders who were born in America.

CHAPTER 15

The weekend appeared in a stormy manner with unpleasent temperatures, Indian weather was making it's day view, soon to disappear. Martha felt restless and frigidity on this long flight and Raheem was not there to comfort her. He left two days ahead of their agreed upon schedule and she had no idea why, however he's just as excited about their trip as she. Wanting very much to be with him, keeping her miserableness concealed and contemplating seriously on their romanced amity. This is her first visit to Africa the motherland and she couldn't wait to gallivant while working on her native language. Romantic thoughts traversed her mind and soul, cogitating on whether or not she should tell him about her pregnancy. She wasn't sure who the father was sneaking off with Raheem three times that week while her and bernard was doing their best to make a baby. Recumbently relaxing as she thought to herself. I know right, I got some nerve being mad at him...I was just as sneaky as he was....but shit he slept with that hooker, and when i inquired about her he lied to me. Fucking her trifling ass in the parking lot of the funeral parlor during my grandmother's wake on top of the car i brought him. Then he allowed her to fuck him in the ass! shit! I was engaged to a homosexual, who hangs out with Floyd the bi-sexual. He was so lovely to me an excellent photographer though the best I had but Mrs. Allred couldn't take it no more catching him for the third time sucking dick on the clock. At least Floyd kept it real, he knew what he liked and didn't like. I don't think Floyd would take pictures of him sleeping with another women, a slut at that,sending them to me. Floyd wouldn't hurt me,shit he tried his best to protect my well being while working for me, and if anything he would get back at Mrs. Allred she fired him not I. Awaiting patiently for the landing of Raheem's private plane, feeling a bit cranky however excited. "Buckle up and prepare yourself for our smooth landing,please," said the aviator. "About time," she said dryly, looking extremely remarkable as ever. Wearing a yellow two-piece long sleeve suit ensemble with v-neck and baby doll collar, five snap closures, two large side pockets and elastic waist mini skirt and black leather mules, by Trenae' Farah. There rested a gold Rolls Royce stretched limosine with four Land Rovers accompanying it and sixteen Nairobi brothers 6'4" in height, 245 pounds of solid weight. "Good evening Miss Jeffries, will you please come with us." One of the huge brothers said resolutely. She felt so honored to have so much attention directed towards her, blushing bashfully. A very large group of spectators waved on as she made hew way to the limo hence waving back. Entering the limo agaped though the atmosphere felt pleasently astonishing to one's heart and soul."Ilove it!" she said emotionally with pride and never seeing such great sights plus beautiful developments. The 110 degree temperature was still rising though the sun beamed strongly on the land leaving heat waves, as they roamed the paved roads. Children jogging alongside of the limo, leaving her very well pleased and doing their best to get a glance at such beauty. Martha felt like a million bucks or more rolling down the window granting her devoted fans beautiful glimpses while thinking to herself. Raheem didn't tell me about the greatness of just being back home and god is definetly in the air over here. I can feel him! I love you too God without a doubt, please give me the strength one need to explore as much of the motherland has to offer. I'mma occupy all our time submissively, now I see why he's over here all the time.

Arriving at what appeared to be a extra large mansion in her eyes, however it was the prince's palace. The Cape Cod style palace has thirty bedrooms in approximately 18,800 square feet. The grey clap board palace has a second floor master suite with large crystal dome trimmed in diamonds facing the ocean. The palace was built in 1940 and had been owned by legendary African King of Kenya, Dorno Bari the father of Prince Dorno Bari the second. The fifteen million dollar palace is surrounded by 1000 acres of land facing the ocean. She couldn't believe her eyes such a beautiful odyssey stared before her, and steady flicking her vectis 2000 minolta camera saying to herself. "Damn this is heaven on earth like the Quaran describes it...mmm...a woman's fantasy."Her mind was not deluding her even though she felt it was this was a special occasion for her. "Raheem you sure know how to wine and dine a girl," trembling from mere excitement as she licks her lips. There were bodyguards everywhere as pulled in the palace's garage.Inside rested ten colorful limosines and twelve colorful rolls royces. To the left of her approximately twenty five horses and a large flourishing stable, each horse wore a gold bracelet on it's gaskins. one of the bodyguards opens the limo door, helping her to her feet and there stood seven beautiful African sisters. Wearing no makeup for she knew these sisters only respect natural beauty and that's something she was born with like them. "Peace sister" said one of them "Peace to you," said Martha nervously. "Relax, you're at home," and Martha does just that from the sound of her voice. She remembers saying the same words to candy when she was nervous from being around such beauty and glamour. Escorting her to a remote room in the palace, "The Princess will be with you shortly so make yourself at home and enjoy your stay my sister....Peace," said the youngest sister of the seven and they all spoke such elegant english. Everyones so amiable and very amenable, "I'm gonna love it here," she yells as she stood amazed at the structure of the room. Six black limestone lions, a double queen size canopy bed trimmed in gold, a large gold mural of the skies and a balcony over looking the ocean. "This is lovely." Walking out on the balcony watching the waves from the waters currents and reminising about her first encounter with Raheem. Wanting so badly to feel the air from the ocean seep through her thighs while making love on the balcony to Raheem. "where is my baby?" she moaned before throwing herself on the bed. The Princess enters the room and in spite of all her excitement she never noticed sprawling over the bed gladsomely. "Enjoying ourselves are we?" Immediately directing her attention towards the sound of the voice and to her surprise there stood a beautiful ebony sister. Dressed in a gold sleeveless roundneck chiffon gown and gold fringed shawl with matching sandals. Diamonds from her head to her toes and those rocks were adorably shining. "Are you ready to perform my darling?" asked the princess. However, Martha was so mesmerized by the fine jewelry she couldn't speak. "My sister, are you okay?" Finally she comes to her senses, "Yes, I'm sorry,I don't know what got into me.""Well let's hope it wasn't an evil spirit." "never that." "We have a load of clothes for you to model, if you care to follow me, I'l show you to your dressing room." Grabbing Martha's right arm and holding it real tight as she walked her to her dressing room. Martha was astonished with the hospitality she was receiving though she felt delighted to be in the presence of royalty not to mention the conversations they were having acting like twin sisters and the princess was real cool. "May i ask you a question?" Martha asked. "Yes go right ahead martha." "Where is my Raheem?" "He's with my husband horseback riding and they won't be back for another hour, just in time for your performance....um....can i share something with you?" "Go right ahead." "My husband has no brothers but he has nine sisters and one wife, that's me." "Can he marry more than one women?" "Yes he can but unfortunetly he wants only one." "So why are you disappointed?" "Oh, I'm not disappointed trust me, but sometimes it's good for a man to have more than one wife if he's wealthy like my prince. Plus a man has alot of obligation that needs to be fulfilled and sometime us woman think we can fulfill them all. that's not the case that's howcome in america the divorce rate is the highest in the world and let's not talk about the single parenting." "So you're saying." "Listen, this is what I"m saying....There are ten females born to every male everyday, only four out of those ten will make it to the heavens and six will make it to hell. Sometime I need privacy but I don't wan to leave my prince alone, so if there was another woman around she can occupy that time when i'm gone....but your Raheem does a wonderful job occupying alot of my prince's time when he visits." "Oh, I get it he's the brother that your prince don't have." "Right!" Galloping away on two black stallion horses alongside the seashore was the Prince and Raheem. "Holddd!" said the prince as he slows his horse down and Raheem does the same, with alot on his mind though his heart felt tortured from love.

"So what do you think I should do?" asked Raheem. "I can't make choices for you but you stay with the one you love the most." "You know Mikasa told me?" "No I don't." "You wasn't suppose to answer that, that was just a figure of speech." "I know bro, it was just a joke," said the Prince with this honest visage. "She can't see herself sharing me with another women especially her ex boyfriend's sister....and you really wanna hear something weird?" "Try me." "I was Martha's first and her brother was my wife's first." "Are you serious?" "I kid you not my prince." "I'mma ask you a serious question you might have to think about it." Stopping both horses before asking him his question, "Who do you love the most, seriously?" Feeling bad inside for he loves Martha more and mikasa"s the one carrying his seeds. "I'm waiting for an answer young man," said the prince curiously. In a veracious manner he said, "Martha i choose for my wife and I love her more than life itself." "Does she feel the same way about you?" "Yes she does." "How do you know?" "I've been sleeping with this woman before my marriage and after." "Are we committing adultery?" "I'm afraid so." "You must stop!"the prince said in a caring manner before telling him the consequences behind that sin. Knowing he had to stop that foul act immediately, that's how come he told mikasa about martha even though he kept their intimacy a secret from everyone."Oh no we're running late we better get going." "Haa!" Raheem yelled as he starts their race back to the palace. "The last man back owes five hundred push-ups." the prince yells strongly.

Thecrowd of natives awaited Martha's presence patiently and knowing they would get their opportunity to meet a beautiful sister born in Jamaica. The runway's surrounded with important guest and fashion designers from all over the world came out to see their tresured goddess. Martha's just as excited as they were modeling infront of royalty even though four amateur models will be accompanying her giving her time to change her outfits. The crowd of spectators were rowdy for a short time and security was tight, these were the king's selectees. Raheem and Prince Dorno made it just in time, for here comes lovely Martha strutting down the runway,wearing a black strapless sequined gown with feather stole and matching heels. It's been awhile since she's walked down a runway however, it was like riding a bike again. One never loses that touch and she felt very comfortable around her native members. Looking extremely remarkable, never letting her fans down and that sexy posture of hers stood out with glamour. Astonishingly all male jaws were hanging, mouths wide opened and hearts palpitating.

Recognising their bashful expressions, spinning and striking sumptuous poses with this bonniful smile. Enticing their hormones, igniting that heated passion inside of them though she was expecting and one would never notice. Making her way back to her dressing room, "Beloved she's georgeously unique and very stunning to one's eyes," said the Prince with this shocking stare."Now you see what i mean." Martha appeared before her audience once again wearing a red body fitted sleeveless shimmering gown with a white fringed evening jacket and matching heels. Applause from the crowd as camers clicked simultaneously, lips licking and egos tripping agape. Steady flossying as she takes these sophisticated strides down the runway, pausing infront of Prince and Raheem spinning thrice before making her way back down the runway to her dressing room. She was definetly a pleaser however, she teased Raheem with a silent buss. "Suitable buxom," whispered the prince, and Raheem sure enough read his lips. "Nifty!" someone yelled. Putting on something more revealing for her fans for she knew she would strike emotions and rise a few manhoods. Raheem though to himself. She won my heart and earned my love, there's nothing I wouldn't do for that woman. Tonight will be a night we will never forget, naked flicks and sexy tricks. Stepping out on the runway was she, wearing a scoop neck sleeveless stretch tulle short cocktail dress with hand sewn swaroviski crystals all over. Catching everyone off guard though they enjoyed the sight of her firm bust, bodacious heart shaped booty and those curvaceous hips with her tenuous smooth legs. She's all a man could want plus more, and impulses were motivated. "Whencesoever you go, I will be there with open arms," Raheem said with tears. He knew Mikasa wasn't interested in sharing him with anyone else, especially Martha. Even though he loved her more and the fact that he was her first made it more challenging. "When you're ready to marry her let me know," said the king. "Why sir?" he asked "My son asked if you can have a royal wedding, and whatever my son ask for he shall receive. He said you are the little brother he's always wanted." Raheem tears grew larger while huging the prince tightly, "Thank you beloved," he cried. "You saved my life for nothing, I will never forget that and as long as God give me life, you will never want for nothing....I love you Raheem," cried the prince and this was definetly an emotional moment for the both of them. The king smiled and said. "Clean those faces, it scares me to see two grown men weeping like children." Pointing at Martha before uttering "You must marry that beautiful princess. If you want a royal wedding my second prince." That's not a problem for him for he wanted to be with her desperately. It was mikasa who frightened him, with her attempts to take her life. The king crowned Raheem after receiving eneryones attention and when he spoke, they listened. Noticing the excitement and wanting to be by his side for a very special moment in his life, unfortunately signing autographs kept her busy. She didn't want to disappoint the natives,after the crowning they rejoiced in harmony and beautiful sisters danced on stage for their new prince and royal family. Dancing very sexually although one of them gives Raheem a very superb belly dance. Up close and personal on her future, starting to feel jealous and wanting very much to intervene unfortunately she didn't. He noticed her spirit and magnificent smiles turned into dejected frowns. In spite of all the excitement from the sexy sisters, he called for her to join in on their cultural celebration. Everything moved in slow motion, her eyes united their hearts and lustful desires. walking towards his table with long strides and hips motionly bouncing , giving a firm grip to her ample backside. Standing as she arrived with his right hand out, and excepting his invitation spiritually silently embracing one another, slow dancing romantically before their spinning around their auras, while the moon shined brightly upon them connecting their silhouette, energizing their emotions.

CHAPTER 16

The great king awarded his newly prince with five hundred million dollars, a hundred acres of pure land with a strong security force of twenty thousand men and his own tribal name. He was admiral in charge of the tribunal, though he works under the first prince, who's the chief veraciously he had the power to build or destroy and knowing of his veritable authority, his men were labled by the American government as the strongest ground troops in the world and highly intelligent. Martha was proud of her prince and wanting very much to do something splendid,even though she spent from her classic works on the runway. Pouring champagne for two jubilantly as he sipped some old brandy, swallowed hard, and said, "Dammnnn!" "Yes honey." "I wasn't talking to you princess...anyway what's taking you so long?" "I'll be out in a couple of seconds." He was definetely chillin in his penthouse over top of his custom designed hotel, the tallest building in the city of Nairobi, Kenya. This stoned twenty five story hotel over looking the Bari River cost a whopping twenty million and this wasn't no flophouse, an exceptionally fine work of art done by Ronnie Farah. Popping in his favorite cd by R. Kelly. He knew exactly what to play to get her out here, switching the channels to his number one song, "If I could turn back the hands of time." when she heard the song she slowly stepped out the master bedroom enticingly wearing a black silk see-through dress; over red snake skin bikini and fishnet stockings with red snake skin garter belt. He had this implausable expression though he loved it, and she looked extremely wonderful, delicious to one's desirers. His heart melts from her heated passion which he absorbs from her delightful aura around that magnificent posture and energetic spirit. Walking towards her slowly, "Baby what the hell!" he said surprising. "You like it?" "like it, I love it!" "I thought you would." Clutching her waist firmly and looking straight into her eyes, he smile and said "Are you ready to bring forth our likeness?" "Yes my prince, but." "But what!" "Nothing." Wanting badly to tell him she's expecting, and wasn't sure who the father is. "Is everything okay?" Raheem asked. "Yes honey." "Well let's get it started, walk over to the lion sofa and do what you do best." she does just that, while he adjusted his Hi-8 Panasonic camera tri-pod. Moving her body sexually on the sofa while he flicks the camera slowly numerous times. "Yes baby......you're doing perfect!" sprawling all over the sofa in a freakish manner was she. Raising her right leg high in the air, removing her fishnet stocking slowly and doing the same to her left leg before spreading her thighs wide. Licking his lips and reminiscing about the tightness of her cunt when squeezeing, milking his every cranny. Crawling slowly so that he can get a better look at her curvaceous hips and tremendous ass. Laying flat one her stomach now, squiriming like a cat in heat before parting her legs and raising just a inch from the sofa. Palming her buttcheeks firmly and removing her snakeskin bikini bottom delicately, granting him a perfect shot of her chocolate ass and fat vagina. The camera's flicking at a speed of forty five miles per second, as his right thumb steadily pressed against it's button. "Remove the top pieces baby." "Now Raheem?" "Yes my love." Removing everything slowly, completely naked before the man she truly loves, dancing in a rhythmical manner shaking her behind erotically sexy and caressing herself. Bending over, swaying her breast and squatting at the same time while he stared lustfully at those beautiful dark chocolate aureoles with thumb size nipples. His manhood grew to an enormous size, stretching his trousers and throbbing was his heart. Ready for penetration and pure satifaction as she walks towards the bed moaning out his name several times, needing that tender action and chain reaction. Her butt was twitching with anticipation and wanting badly to feel his nature inside of her. Walking towards the bed slowly and removing his trousers, now standing before her naked with this daring smile. Unexpectedly her eyes opened wider from eagerness and glossy reflection developed. Their undying love for one another filled the air creating a strong aura of ecstasy. "Comeeeee," she moaned spiritually and her eyes revealed the heaven to her soul. Spreading her legs widely, as he crawled between them, licking her belly button to the center of her bosom slowly, and meeting her lips invading her already opened mouth. Twin tears rolled down her cheeks not from sorrow, however from a strong soulfully electrifying moment. Feeling the urge to climax before he even slid his God given nature into her womb of generations. Stentorian sounds of pleasure seeped her throat, leaving her vagina succulently moist. The moon's full of God's Glory and so were they, osculating and caressing. Whispering his name through her lips. Regulate. She has never felt this stimulation inside of her ever, and she remebered their first encounter like if it was yesterday, however right now feels better.

CHAPTER 17

Taking care of business as usual was Pretty Tony, "All this damn paper work....shit, where the fuck is Martha?" he raved. She was home relaxing from a plendid weekend with the love of her life. "Sandy." "Yes Mr. Handley The Third." "Get intouch with Miss Jeffries for me and tell her I need her signature in order to mail these advertisements out." "Okay sir, I'll get right on it." "Yeah you do that," he utters dryly. Talking on her speaker phone jubilantly, "Girl it was lovely." "Was it?" "Yes it most certainly was." "I'm happy for you Martha." "I know Yasha." "So yall had an African engagement?" "Sure did and they crowned us with land and money." "Over there?" "Yes honey!" "So are you leaving us soon?" "No...cause I'm taking yall with me." "Girl I don't know if i wanna live in Africa." "Don't worry baby you're gonna love it plus Raheem wants yall with us." "What about our businesses and other family members?" "We have one hundred acres of land." "What!?" "I kid you not." "Damn that's enough for four tribes." "More than that girl and my husband is building me a five story office building over looking the Bari River....so we can work from there." "Did you tell Tiffany yet?" "Yes I did." "And what did she say?" "She's ready to leave, hold on a minute someone is at my door." "You know how I feel about the hold on, go ahead and handle your business while I prepare dinner for my baby." "Give the family my love." "I will,bye!" "Bye!" she had video cameras specially delivered to her home and pretty tony's her next project. Setting up the equipment while contemplating on her future event with pretty tony and tonight will be very offensive.

Receiving a urgent telegram from someone he wanted so badly even though they weren't ready to tempt his emotions. "What took you so long wench?" he snarled as he prepared for a so called romantic evening with his dream girl. Eventhough he had no idea of the telegrams deceitfullness. "Sandy, tell my wife I won't make it for dinner because i have alot of paperwork to attend to." "Yes sir! I'll get right on it." "Did you get intouch with Martha?" "No sir." "Alright, forget about her for now just call my wife." "Will do sir."

Hours later.......Floyd arrives at Martha's home with this dumfounded look and acting like a dunce. "So glad you could make it." "How have you been Martha?" he said femininely. "Okay and yourself." "The usual." "The cameras are waiting for your professional touch....here's your check." "Thank you darling, I can use this quarter of a million dollars." "Just remember stay hidden until he leaves, okay?" "Yes sugar cakes."....Meanwhile Tony jumps into his brand new Sky blue Testerosa immediately rushing to his destruction. Martha found out about Tony's snooping around and picture taking of Bernard's slutful affair. Thinking to herself;I got everything ready....let me check again: Champagne, snacks, and music. Well Pretty Tony today is your day and tonight is your night , you deserve the best. The doorbell rings, "Floyd are you ready?" Martha whispered meticulously. "Yes darling, I believe so." Answering the door aplumb. "Hey Pretty tony." she whispered enticingly. Wearing a mint green instant body shaping bra slip. Admiring her beauty as usual, he grants her a wet kiss . Surprisingly accepting his quick uncontrollable emotions behind her seducive hug and gentle rub on his penis. Pulling back before spinning and allowing him a perfect stare at that ample ass she hauled. Gripping her buttocks firmly, "oooo! Tony not so hard babyyy."Escorting him to her velour sofa, as she pours him a drink he said, "What made you give in?" "Your sweet charm and big prick." handing him his drink before caressing that enormous bulge in his trousers. "You feel ready,"Martha whispered shrewdly. "Are you surprised?" "No, not really but I don't know if I'm doing the right thing." "Don't worry you're doing the right thing and besides who's gonna find out? Are you gonna tell on yourself? I know I'm not." Laying back on the sofa and lying on top of her between her legs was he. While loving every minute of it he softly fondles her breast and vagina, leaving her emotionally enticed. Knowing she had a job to do kept her focused and steadfast.

Being very submissive to his warm embrace at least that's what Floyd thought as he stared thru the lens of the video camera stupidly. Tony started getting out of control, sucking her breast frantically while forcefully ramming his index finger in her vagina. Thinking to himself. This hot bitch deserves everything I'mma about to do to her, roughly without remorse. He's being very impious and she recognizes it. "Tony what the hell are you trying to do to me?"she barked "Fuck you like you wanna be fucked!" "Did you leave your wife yet?" "No, but after tonight that bitch is history." "How do i know you're telling the truth?" "Because after receiving your telegram I called her and explained everything to her." "Did you baby?" "Yes, I did sweety." Licking the finger he stuck in her womb sensually, "OOO, aren't we freaky." she utters. That's Floyd's cue, immediately dialing her number on his cellphone.Ringing stentorianly."Excuse me Tony, I must answer that." "No Martha let it ring." "I can't I'm expecting an important call, business first and pleasure last. Don't worry I'm not going anywhere and neither are you." Walking to the phone while provctively wobbling that immense ass of hers. He couldn't take no more, his heart's beating rapidly from mere excitement. Martha's speaking in a fortissimo manner. "No! Your husbands not here!" Tony over heard what appeared to be an angry conversation with her and his wife. "Oh God!" he said as his visage went from appealing to ghastly. "You better not bring your ass over here hussy!" wasting no time he immediately vamooses out the front door. Hanging up the phone mischievously and laughs her head off. Not taking any chances pulling out of her driveway crazily for he knew she would come over there with the gun and blast them both without hesitation. "Tony wait!" she yells joyfully. He paid her no mind however he left his wallet and that's more than enough evidence to convict him. Floyd couldn't help himself, holding his stomach while laughing simultaneously. "You're crazy girl." "I knowFloyd and I trully thank you for your expertisse." "Anytime darling-anytime, I can use the extra work and money, honey!" Escorting him to the door, at this time Bernard drives up and parked across the street.

In plain view of her front porch and wanting eagerly to knock on her door. Missing her very much and having nightmares for weeks about their departure. Opening the door slowly as Floyd exits the house." Martha girl you're the best, can I have some sugar before I leave." "Boy have you been sucking penis this week?" "Now bitch don't go there!" "I know I'm not hearing you correctly!" "Yes you is MRS.BITCH! and I hope you're not getting new on me!" "No I'm not Floyd and I deeply regret saying that." "You hurt my feelings girl!" wearing this discombobulated look and dropping his head. "Come here boy and give mommy some sugar." "On the lips?" "Yes." Puckering up was she as their lips united and Floyd definetly felt a warm sensation flowing thru his body. Staring on was Bernard with this ominous expression and neither one of them noticed. A friendly kiss turned thriller. "So he's behind all this bullshit I've been going thru.Wanting Martha all the time, you son of a bitch and look what she has on......let the world know you're fucking him bitch! Coming outdoors looking like a tramp! How could he betray me like that?I trusted his fuckin ass and he set me up with that young stinkin ass harlot so he could get my furture wife," Bernard babled. "Take care delicious,"Floyd said as he enters his Gold Jeep Grand Cherokee Limited.Shutting her door swiftly, making her way to her bedroom very exhausted and feeling like a starlet all over again. Following Floyd as he dials his jeep phone. "Hello!" "What's up floyd?" "What's up Bernard,you're up kinda late." "Yeah man I couldn't really sleep." "How did you know I was in my jeep?" "I tried the house first." "Oh alright, so what's on your mind?" "Where you headed too or coming from?" "This bitch house, who's been stressing me all week." Never aware that Bernard's trailing him and knowing the bitch he's talking about, atleast that's what he thinks. "Who is this bitch?" Bernard asked "You don't know her anyway." "try me." "Cindy." "Never heard of her." "I know you haven't." "Well i"mma get some sleep now.""You do that." "See you later Floyd,bye!" CLICK! "Damn he acted like a police with his hundred questions, bullshit!"

Later on that evening approximately seven o clock p.m. Martha was sound asleep looking sexy as ever wallowing under her gold stin sheets buttnaked. little did she know of the confusion that was about to take place with bernard and her dear friend......Dialing his number slowly while contemplating on his devilish acts and evil desires that hovered his heart. The phone rings several times and no one answers. "Girl would you lighten up on the cocain before you bust your heart." "Please Floyd! I know what i'm doing" Barbara said, though she continued sniffing heavily."If you die in here no one will ever know!because i'mma drag your ass out to the curb." "You better listen to him Barbara," said Twany while waving his hands and snapping his fingers, he screams "You go girl!" "Shut the fuck up you homo!" she barked. "Listen Bitch!my name ain't madonna and i ain't a material girl living in a material world. So stop stricking poses like a bitch and be the man you were born to be!" "You got some nerve!you dyke bitch! running around here sucking more pussy than a fisherman selling fish with the f.d.a. approval." "What you mean f.d.a. approval?" "Funky dyke association!" "No you didn't!" "Yes i did miss dyke bitch!" Intervening was Floyd, "Get out of my way Floyd...I'mma beat the dick out that nigger ass,"Barbara barked. "Step out the way Floyd," as he snaps two fingers in the air,"Because ain't nothing between us but air and fish bait!" Twany said angrily. "Listen at that chick with a dick, your heart better be as big as your asshole, cocksucker!" Floyd started laughing profusely,"Would you both stop the nonsense, so what you like pussy and he like dick.....I like them both," he said sweetly. "Oh lord girl , we better not get him started," Twany utters simultaneously while laughing.

Sipping on some old whiskey, swallowed hard and said,"I know he's home...why don't he answer?" "Hello!" "What's up Floyd?" "Who's this?" "Nigger you forgot my voice?" "Oh, Bernard what can I do for you good buddy?" "I need to see you." "Now?" "Yes!" "This is the wrong time man, I'm enjoying myself." "I thought our friendship was tighter than that." "It is man but I'mma 'bout to get my freak on." "I'm sorry but I really need to see you." A moment of silence seeps thru the phone and Floyd was really pondering on helping a friend or getting his doggy-style on. "Okay Bernard come over." "Thanks Floyd you are a true friend." "Yeah,yeah just get your ass over here because i don't have all night." "I'm on my way." Click! Floyd was really upset that he had to stop his enjoyment for a few hours though he was ready for some licking and sticking. "Excuse me darlings, yall have to get missing for about two hours.""What honey!" said Twany boisterously. "Bernard's coming over for an advising conversation." "Now?" Barbara blurted. "It won't be long yall I promise...... here take my jeep keys and get missing." "Shit man, my assholes twitching for your hard prick Floyd." "And so is my pussy baby,"Barbara cried before cuffing that bulk in his trousers, while Twany planted his penis on Floyd's ass, sandwiching him were them both. "Come on guys stop it, get going please bring my jeep back in one piece."

At Tiffany's mansion in Kingston, Jamaica......."Would you boys please stop fighting." "NOOOO!" "Father!" "Yes love." "Would you please attend to the boys, they are not listening to me." Immediately they stop the nonsense, however Father was in no position at this time to chastise anyone. He's busy preparing an important presentation. Leaving the boys with their nanny. "I'll take them Tiffany," said Tarah. "Thank you so much." slowly walking towards the den, opening the door quietly, "Uh-huh I see you," Tiffany whispers. "I know you do." Giving him a romantic massage on those broad shoulders he very well possessed. "How this feels?" she asked. Grabbing her hand, kissing it simultaneously while seating her on his lap. "You're the best Tiff." "I know baby and so are you... what is that poking me?" "You know what that is." "Are you giving me a hint?" "Something like that." "Do you have time?" "Why you ask?" "Because I don't wanna disturb your work." "You are my work," he whispers as he fondles her body."OOOH,YEAHHHH!" "Is the door locked?" "Yes it is Father." "Aren't we anticipating my actions." "That's my job to know when my husband needs it and wants it." Sticking his tongue in her mouth and slurping up all her hot saliva slowly. This was one heated moment and Tiffany's loving every minute of it, though her fetus moved around swiftly knowing daddy would be knocking at it's door.

Arriving at the door step of Floyd's mini mansion. "I'm coming Bernard!" "I know you are fool." Bernard was drunk as a skunk and ready to release some stress though he's been feeling very aggravated. Opening the door agog was Floyd with this gawk look. "Come in Bernard." Walking in without a smile on his face and Floyd knew something was definetely wrong. Giving off this unusual aura and negative vibe, "Wanna drink?" Floyd asked nervously. "Yeah, why not." Walking over to the bar alertly and pouring him a glass of gin accommodatingly. "What can i do for you good buddy?" he asked sincerly. "give me another shot of gin for starters...i have a few questions i need answered." "Sure buddy, I'll do my best to answer them." Bernard looked as if he hadn't had sleep for days,growing a beard and bags hung from beneath his eyes. "You know I love Martha very much don't you?" "Not really, i thought you bypassed her by now." "I bet you did." "What you mean by that Bernard?" "I don't know you tell me." "Tell you what?" Pulling out his thirty eight and pointing it directly at floyd's chest. Floyd's eyes expanded from fear and not knowing what to say, however finding some emergency words, immediately he said "Man what's gotten in to you?" Sounding like a bitch bernard thought. He started showing all of his feminin ways and it was written all over his face. His body actions appeared strange in Bernard's eyes as he dropped to his knees. "Please don't kill me,I'll do anything you want.....want me to suck your dick?" "What?" Bernard blurted with this omen stare. "You're gay too?" "Yes but, I was gonna tell you soon." "When, next year motha'fucka?!" "Pleas don't kill me!" Bernard thought to himself. He's a homo fucking my Martha and he's probably been fucking her from the first day he met her. Being her personal photographer in all for two years and they were very close,to close for me. How blind could i have been advancing his ass in his profession while he advanced his dick in Martha. All Bernard visions flashed before him and the main one was him killing Martha romantically, and she practically had on nothing. His eyes were firey red with tears. "I hate to do this but you leave me no choice," Bernard whispered hatefully. Floyd became speechless, seeing the angel of death left him terrified and emotionally disturbed. Hearing two gun shots as they entered his chest painful and swiftly. Blood squirted abundantly, simultaneously Bernard impassively walked out the front door and slowly entering his car before vanishing from the scene. Crawling to his death and doing his best to reach his phone, however no luck. In deep agony as his body was covered in blood, writing what appeared to be three letters with his blood before collapsing to his death.

The winds traveling roughly, the inclement weather's creating a livid after effect. Martha tossed and turned all night, no nightmares though feeling uncomfortable as the fetus inside her kept swimming back and forth. Yasha was watching her favorite movie, Awakening To Misery by Raheem Farah. Loving this movie dearly, leaving her very emotional and eyes full of tears with two boxes of kleenex. This film's definetely controversial,events based on true reality,however people weren't ready to face the tragedies that go on everyday in our societies.Farah productions brought veraciousness to the world with this film, and competitors were doing their best to discredit his writers. The movie accumulated a whopping four hundred and twenty five million dollars in two weeks time.

CHAPTER 18

SIX MONTHS LATER, Raheem stared in tears at the platinum vase which rested Mikasa's ashes. The superstar singer died last week while giving birth too twin girls. In time of need Martha comforts her Prince and in the publics eyes,she's his chaperone,even though that wasn't the case. The authorities were looking for Floyd's killers, having no luck at this time and the deceased family were pressuring them. Looking over the photos that were taken of the crime scene. "Detective Ricky." "Yes Cathy." "I've been going over these photos for weeks." "And!.." "I just came across something that we over looked." "What's that?!.." "Some initals on the end of the sofa." "Let me see that." Observing what appeared to be three letters which read ber. "Ber!..."shouted detective Ricky. "Is that what it say?" "Yes partner." "Are you sure?" "Sure as a rat's ass." Receiving the case some weeks ago, in spite of all the contraversy thats been lingering around this ordeal. Being awarded the opportunity to solve what some might say, and impossible murder. These homicide detectives were from another state,however, always catching their culprit and serving justice with out hesitation. Solving twenty five of the world's oldest murder mysteries. Neither detective was married, dedicating all of their time to their work and in spite of the long trips, they were able to fulfill eachothers needs physically,mentally and spiritually. "Cathy." "Yes Ricky." "Lets go visit the place of execution." "Good idea." Wanted for the murder were Barber and Twany, their finger prints were found all over the place. "Barber and Twany are living in the Farah hotel." "Which one?"Asked Ricky. "The one on Boston road." "Thank you very much." CLICK!..Driving calmly were the both of them,Ricky looked at Cathy surprisingly and said,"baby this is the first time a precinct out of our jurisdiction has cooperated with us." Are we surprised?" "Yes i am." "Don't be." Twany was fast asleep though he grieved the whole six months after Floyd's death, and loving him more than life itself. Barbra's escaping her grief by getting high and her habit grew stronger, sniffing three ounces a day finding their best friend stretched out in a pool of blood, dead as a door knob,horrified their hearts. They didn't know if Bernard did this or not,consequently afraid of his wealth and power lead them on the run for six months,knowing they were not the murders. Arriving at the Farah hotel with plain clothes on. "Excuse me." "Yes sir may i help you?" Showing his badge before saying,"Yes you can help me,we just got word that some fugitives are hiding here." "Oh no!" "Please lady don't get hysterical on me,calm down." Mean while Cathy cases the place and called for back up. Barbra comes out for ice,leaving the door open and Cathy sneaks in. Waving to her partner,letting him know that Barbra's at the ice machine. Swiftly he moves with his gun out creeping behind her,while placing the barrel on the back of her head... "Freeze!!..."he whispered. "We didn't kill him!"she cried nervously. "I know yall didn't...but...we still need your help to catch the real killer." Shoving Twany twice,leave me Barbra,"he mutters spently. shoving him once again,though this time he awakes angrily to a forty five automatic pointed directly at his nose,hence screaming like a bitch. "It wasn't meeeee!.."

Martha's preparing for her wedding next month, having a guest list up to two thousand family members and friends. Purchasing a custom made white suede bodice empire gown with gold trimming and matching shoes,by Trenae' Farah. The cost of such wear, four hundred thousand dollars,this was the first wedding gown designed by FARAH'S DESIGNERS,and it's selling like hot cakes. Raheem's doing his best to get over his first wife's death, though he enjoyed spending time with his beautiful daughters and having one of his native sister's suckle them until they reach the age of knowing right from wrong. The precinct's crowed with news reporters,Lawyers and nosy spectators. Cathy did her best ,addressing the reporters with a frivolous story and adumbrated show. Ricky on the other hand was admonishing the so call suspects. "Look at these photos real good and tell me what you see!"he raved Starting to get on his nerves,he yelled. "Listen, the D.A. wants your fucken heads!..Now if yall loved Floyd like you say ,help me and i'll help you...you have my word on that." They were in great fear and he knew this by their expressions. "I can't stand to look at them photos any-more,"cried Twany bitchly. However, Barbra couldn't take the verbal abuse,his interrogation drove her crazy. "Bernard did it!"she yelled with lots of tears racing down her fat cheeks. Ricky immediately shows her the photos with the initials,B.E.R. "Do you think your friend was doing his best to write his killers name before he died?" "I think so officer Ricky." "Why would Bernard wanna kill him?" "I have know idea but he called Floyd that night while we were partying and Floyd told us to get missing for two hours." "Why?" "He didn't want his other friends to know that he had another world he indulged in." "And what world is this." A moment of silence hovered the room. "The gay world,"she said while dropping her head to her knees in tears. "Come young lady you're doing good,don't give up now." Ricky utters as he waved the other officers out the room. "Barbra!" "Yes officer Ricky...I'm still here." "Were you doing drugs?" "Yes i was." "were they doing drugs?" "Yes they were." "Where can we find this Bernard Fella?" "All i know is that he owns a modeling agency,and they all work for Farah productions." "Thee,Farah productions!" "Yes." "Damnnn!" "What?"Twany blurted. "I'm tired of bring down these rich,fucks,...Who think their money can buy them freedom and happiness." Two hours later Tony's wife received a large package,federal express first class. Chillin in his office was Tony, and Martha storms in with out knocking. "Hey Martha!" "Don't hey Martha me...you lying,piece of shit!" Tony stood in anger. "Sit your quater ass down before i make change.." HE does just that, as she walked around his desk,ass jumping in those tight denim Farah jeans. "How dare you leave me like you did,"she ravel. "I had no chiice." "Shut up,I didn't ask for you to talk...my cunt was aching for some love,and yo' bitch ass ran out on me with out any explanation." "Martha I'll make it up to you." "Oh no!..there wont be a next time." Turning around,giving him her back,and standing in a akimbo way,she said,"Take one last look at what could have been yours." He stood slowly wrapping his arms around her petite waist, not sure of her reactions,however,he takes a chance. Allowing him the comfort of rectitude,as she wiggled a little bit and he enjoyed the plumpness of her buttcheeks relaxing on his penis. Throwing her head back meeting his broad chest and shoulder. "Tony I want you so bad before i get married,but i'm afraid Raheem will find out and destroy you afterwards,"she moaned softly. Putting him in a trance before allowing him the opportunity to caress her breast and vagina. Removing his hand from her vagina.. "No Tony,"she whispered,"go home to your wife baby...give her some gooddd loving,we'll deal with eachother later." Removing herself from his warm embrace while he stood confused,with this ridiculous stare. "Tony!" "Yes." "I hope i see you again in one piece,"she said sarcastically while blowing him a death kiss,and slamming his door behind her. His phone rings six times before he answered it. "Hello!" "Hello honey." "Oh Thelma, it's you." "Who else did i sound like?" "No one darling, this phone needs a little fixing." "Honey i got rid of the children and i'm making you a candle light dinner,but you must come home early." "Are you feeling a little freaky." "Alittle ain't the word." after what Martha just did he surely needed some physical affection. "I'm on my way sugar dumpling,"he said romantically. "Don't rush,i don't want for you to get into a car accident." "Don't worry about that,just stay hot like you are." "Oh i will trust me." He knew he had to get home quick before she changes her mind. They haven't had sex in two months,her career came first and she traveled much.

Inside the underground parking lot the forty five story main-Executives office building,owned and designed by Farah Enterprise waiting patienty for the valet,as he drives up in her brand new 2000 pink custom made Ferrari F355 2door. "Here you go mrs. Bari,"said the valet excitingly with a smile. "Why thank you Roy." "You are most certainly welcome mada'm." Smiling from ear to ear was Martha,as she entered her car and Roy shuts the door with respect. Driving off slowly,looking extremely sexy and glowing healthily. Stopping at a red light, awaiting it's change sluggishly, for she was depleted of energy and today was the busiest day of her life, lots of paper work. Relocating her business head quarters to Africa took alot of doing physically and mentally. Being very excited about her marriage to the second Prince of Nairobi,Kenya and anxiously awaiting that glamourous wedding next month, with her and Raheem. Receiving the second Princess crown by the Queen of Nairobi. The crown cost ten million dollars,made in Egypt,solid platinum decorated with Diamonds and valuable gems. Looking thru her rearview mirror several times before noticing that someone was trailing her. Dialing for security immediately while saying to herself."Who the hell is this following me." "Hello Farah security." "Yes this is

Mrs.Bari." explaining to them her problem in a frantic manner,"Calm down Mrs. Bari, we have a jeep following you at all times...Be patient they will handle the situation." "Thank you." "You-welcome our fine Princess." Hanging up her car phone smoothly,though she prayed for it not to be Bernard in spite of all the pain he's put her through emotionally and spiritually.

sticking his key in the door's lock, opening automatically for she knew of his presence and to his surprise there stood his wife dressed in all black,and her negligee was definitely enticing...Looking extremely dainty. He couldn't believe his eyes,as he stood agape with his heart beating rapidly. "Come in honey and close the door,"she whispered solemnly. Doing exactly that before granting him with a sluttish and slyly kiss. "Honey whats gotten into you?"he asked concernly. Knowing something's wrong or strange,though she's never acted like this, thinking to himself. Here's a woman who prayed before having sex and now she looks like a prostitute or a married man's mistress. May be she bumped her head catching amnesia or could it be that she's pleasing me because i disagreed with her two week trip to Germany,even though it was business...Well fuck it who really cares,not i, i'll just enjoy the moment. Answering his question playfully mischievous,"A little devilishment, why don't you like it?" "I love it." "I bet you do,"she whispered roguishly while wrapping her arms around his neck,pinning him against the wall and lifting her right leg,so that bulge in his trousers can rub against her beautiful pubic hairs. Hating herself dearly for doing this,going out of her character to please a no good man,she thought to herself. Hiring a private investigator to watch his ever move and finding out .that she was married to a philander hurted her soul. blaming herself for his action lefted her vile and confused twelve years of loyalty gone to hell, adultery and fornication on his part only. What's a modest woman to do this was the first and only man she's ever been with, her childhood sweet heart turn sour. Massaging her beautiful buxom,and swiftly tearing off his garments like a wild beast. With this flabbergast-Expression Tony said."Don't stop!..I wanna see all the freak come out of you but take it slow baby." Doing just that,stepping back dancing like a topless dancer,rubbing her vagina and breast like a gelsha in heat. Bending over,spreading her legs and parting her buttcheeks,granting him a direct stare at her fat juice cunt. He was loving all of her astonishing activities. Walking towards her and sweeping her off her feet as he caried her to their bedroom. The clouds grew near,bringing forth inclement weather with loud and forceful thunder bolts. Laying her softly on the bed looking deeply into her eyes before he said. "I love you." "Do you Tony?" "Yes i truly do." Rolling over on top of him was she,"Let me make you feel good baby,"she said emotionally. Mounting herself,as she slides down on his manhood slowly,and pleasingly wiggling from mere intensity. Sweat dripping profusely as she palms his immense chest while cogitating on her next- instantaneous move. Reclining in her leather recliner reading her favorite book, 'JINNS' written by her husband the great original author Raheem. Wearing a pink lace sheath night gown,her husband's favorite color, though he's out the country for a few days on business. Martha kept herself busy ,however,she was lonely,gaining alot of weight from that fetus inside of her and wanting badly to know who's the father... Ecstasy's in the air as they sexual satiated one another and bouncing even more frantically on his pole until he shot his hot nature in her wet juicy cunt causing her womb to ovulate a massive mucilage. Collapsing on him spently and reaching underneath the pillow,grabbing that new nickle plated thirty eight revolver. "How was it baby?"she asked. He could barely respond though he said joyfully. "Thats the best sex we've ever had and we made three children together." "So you loved it?" "Did i,shit!..I want some more." "Closing his eyes with this big smile like if he's in heaven,totally the opposite of where he's about to go. Rising slowly once again while wiggling her hips rhythmly to a old song she hummed. Tears trailing down her twin cheeks as she pointed the gun between his eyes and said."Tony,you are a worthless piece of shit!!!" Opening his eyes to see gun sparks and hearing one loud sound. Brains splattered everywhere and blood smacks her chest and face. Opening her mouth swiftly,and pulling the trigger blowing her uvula to smithereens. Love is the highest flower of emotion and if humans was to be endued with emotions,those emotions could lead them to the highest and drag them to the lowest. The power of will or choosing would have to go with them in order that we may steer our own bark. Mrs. Handely loved her husband more than life itself and being a frim believer to the saying,to death do us apart. Thats exactly what she does though he wasn't worth her life. Leaving behind three lovely young children,two girls and a boy. From top to bottom Tracy twelve,Brandy ten and Tony jr. five. This will be some very emotional times for Mr.Handley the first and family. Awakening to that lovely sound of her alarm clock, while stretching that healthily plump and ample of figure. Wearing a pink satin sheath night gown and hair hanging below her shoulder blades looking extremely sexy. Turning on her large wall screen T.V. watching the news every morning before going to work was her regular. A speacial bulletin appeared and there stood two reporters with these deplorable expression infront of pretty Tony's mansion, as others, rolled out two body bags. Immediately giving all of her attention to this terrible tragedy for she knew one of those bags were filled with Tony's body. One of the reporters said," A unpleasant dilemma has struck us today, Mr. and Mrs. Handley was found this morning in their master bedroom of their mansion with gun shot wounds,which lead to their deaths." "Yes,you're absolutely correct Rob...They were found by their house keeper,who notified police immediately.That's all we have at this time,and the authorities have the slightest idea of what happened,"said the other reporter. "Back to you Bill." "Yes folks,hopefully we'll have more information later this evening on this terrible event. Here in our news rooms,the cast and all employees send our deepest condolenceses to the Handley family. We'll be right back with more channel R news,after a word from our sponsors." Martha stared at the screen stunned and regretful,never wanting Mrs.Handley to take her own life. She just wanted her to know what type of husband she had. Hoping she would divorce him,taking everything he owned because he deserved misfortune. Groggily walking towards her bathroom with this vile gaze,feeling responsible for that solemnly tragedy. Filling her palms with water, splashing slowly on her face before staring in the mirror melancholy. Thinking to herself. Damn Martha what are you doing? This is not you and you know better. I'll give the children a million dollars a piece and start a benefit in their cause. She knew if she didn't do this her conscience would get the best of her, evil nightmares and all. However, her main target was destroyed once and for all, though deserving his destruction in spite of what she thought, the children will suffer the most behind this shameful incident. Calling her office and telling them she wasn't coming in today while trudging back to her bed she received a sharp pain in her lower right leg. Seating herself slowly, glaring at her ankles and they were very swollen and the doctor warned her to stay off her feet. However, stubborness got the best of her, being very immensed from her pregnancy left her vexed at times. Praying underneath her breath. "God please,please, please, forgive me....I promise, I'll make sure those children are well protected. Give me the strength to forgive myself for participating in such a cruel act.Don't curse me and my baby, give me time to repent for my sins. Holding her stomach while saying these words:"My heart's tender and my soul's barricaded at least that's how I feel. Banished from true reality until I'm with Raheem....my love, one and only love. I wanna come back home, my Lord. I've been mistreated by the material world, I've fallen victim to money and power with little respect for myself and those around me...." Dropping her head disgracefully in tears, although her whole life flashes before her, the past and present. Who knows what the future may bring besides GOD, well,... we can find out if one reads on with an open mind.......

CHAPTER 19

Arriving at Bernard's mansion impassively, were the two brilliant detectives. Bernard was busy entertaining a beautiful young model from his agency and she was only seventeen years old, however her body was of a grown woman. "Here daddy let me do that," she moaned. Small grunts seeped his throat as he allowed her to mount apon his lap, while relaxing in his recliner. Feeding him grapes slowly, wearing a sheer red satin jersey gown with nothing up under it, red garter belts and red high heel pumps. Looking vigorously sexy with that humongeous back bone and petite waist. Massaging her breast gently though he knew she was under aged he didn't care,plus she just took twenty nude photos for his new porn magazine. Ricky was busy snooping around looking thru Bernard's livingroom window. At this time Cathy acknowledges his actions before smacking him upside the head she said. "Would you ring the bell already and stop that because we don't have a search warrant." "We don't need one for guys like him." "Oh i see, you wanna blow this case don't you?" "No! I wanna blow his ass." "You sound a little tense....maybe we need to take a long vacation after this one." "I wouldn't mind if we do." Staring at one another romantically before ringing the bell. Squeezing her butt firmly."Stop that!" she said. "Now who the fuck is this!" Bernard asked boisterously. "I don't know daddy." "I know you don't know sugar, however daddy's gotta take care of some business. Now go wait in the den and keep that thing hot for me." She rose slowly and said. "After you get rid of our interruption, will you please fuck my thight pussy?" "I'mma do more than that, now get going." Walking away slowly as her tight black booty twitched with anticipation leaving him very aroused."Dammnnn!" he said before answering his door. "Excuse me sir don't mean to disturb you," Cathy said. "Oh don't worry about that, what can i do for you?" Allowing them to enter, though he had know idea who they were or what they wanted.Walking over to his bar and said."Care for something to drink?It's top of the line." "No thank you, were on duty." "Are y'all police?" "Yes, we are, Homicide detectives." Changing his whole demeanor and Ricky observed his body language carefully as it went from relaxing to unpleasentness. "Do you care if we ask you a few questions?" asked cathy. "No, go right ahead, I have nothing to hide." "Where'd you go last night?" "Where'd i go?" Bernard seemed confused for a minute. "Say bozo, where were you last night?" Ricky asked angrily. "I was home all night." "With who?" "None of your business." "Perhaps we will have to take you in." "Are you arresting me?" "Not at this time." "Well then I think you should leave." The room became quiet and both men glared at one another. She acknowledges Ricky losing it, though he loved bringing down rich guys, especially the ones who thought they were untouchable. "May i ask you a question?" she asked softly. "Yes you may, you beautiful young lady." Ricky immediately stepped forward when he said that, however, she came between them. "You better be glad she stepped infront of me."Ricky raved. "No, I think it's the other way around!" Bernard sneered. "Mr. Hall do you know Floyd Fisher?"she asked. He scowled,"I don't know what's going on.I feel like i'm being manipulated, and i don't like it. it scares me." "I hope it do...life behind bars is where you belong."Ricky said. "Hold up....hold up...tell me what is this all about, anyhow?" "Listen you cocksucker! Floyd was found shot to death in the livingroom of his home, and to our surprise, your initials were written in blood on his sofa....did you or did you not make a phone call to him the night of his death?" "I don't know what you're talking about." "Oh yes you do.....don't get amnesia on me now, it's too late for that...Read this!" Handing him a photo copy of Floyd's phone bill. "So what does this mean?" Bernard asked. "It means you were the last person to call that house a hour before the murder." "I'm not going to stand for this, get out!" "Oh, we'll be back and do us a big favor, don't try to leave the states..we'll find you." "I have no reason to run." "you have more than enough reason to run. I think you should call matlock for this one...let's go cathy!" Slamming his door behind them."You think he's gonna leave?" she asked. "Most likely he will." "well, we better watch him." "That's already logged in my mind." "Baby you can be so harsh at times." "Gotta be with these guys." "I love it though." "I know you do." Bernard was extremely nervous, not knowing what to do. Pouring another drink before calling his young doll, though he knew deep down inside he had to leave the country."Yes daddy you called for me?" He sipped his scotch, swallowed hard, and said,"Are you ready for your big break?" "Yes daddy i'm ready." "Go upstairs and prepare yourself for your first movie." Hot like a firecracker as she sashayed up the steps. He was about to make a real movie and his star would be that beautifully lovely seventeen year old, though she was ready for anything. She would give her life to be a movie star, and he convinced her the best way he knew how, money, drugs, and lies.

Meanwhile Barbara and Twany were being watched under heavy observation, secured by Illinois's finest.It's eight o' clock a.m. The alarm rang loudly. Barbara's heads was hurting and she awoke cursing. "Stupid will you turn off that loud ass alarm?!" receiving no response. The alarm continued to scream. "Twany!" she yelled into his sleeping ear, "Turn off that loud shit! Wake up bitch!" she began shaking him, "Wake the fuck up, shit head!.....are you dead!"Twany slowly emerged from his stupor. Reaching for the clock slowly, jumping merrily on the nightstand close to the bed, and locating it, pushed the small lever back into it's silent zone. Barbara watched him disgustedly."Girl what are you doing up so early?" "I'm hungry!" "Calm down." "Give me some money!"   "That's   what   ya'   silly   ass   woke   me   up   for?" Yeah why?" "Look in my suit jacket, I think there's four hundred dollars in the inside pocket.""You think, bitch you don't get paid to think.""Would you retrieve the money bulldog, and leave me the hell alone....disturbing my beauty sleep.""You call what you display beauty...ha...well, i'mma ask GOD to do the world a favor." "And what's that miss wench?" "Keep yo' ass asleep forever." "You got some nerve you!....girl don't start with me this morning, it's too early for the bullshit."

His heart's aching, his mind confused and nerves jumping badly. He needed to talk to someone, unfortunately he only knew of one person he could truly trust. Dialing the number slowly and praying that this was the right one. Cutting in on Martha's conversation:"Hello,Tiffany." "Hi Martha." "Who is this?" "A dear friend." "A dear friend....excuse me, you have to be more specific because I have lots of friends and fans." "I miss you so much," he sounded so torn apart, however she still couldn't make out the voice. "Give me a second." clicking over to see if Tiffany was still there. "She musta got lost again.Oh well, she call back soon." Tears rolling down his cheeks, he's to far gone and needing salvation. "I'm back. now who is this?" inquired

Martha piously. "Ah, hell, maybe i better go." Recognizing his voice. "Bernard is that you?" "I..I....just thought I'd call." She was happy to hear from him, however, never wanting him to know that. "How have you been." she asked concerly. "The truth or a lie." silenced for a moment. "Bernard you sound terrible." "I feel terrible." "Is there anything i can do for you?" "Yes...hear me out."He knew of her pregnancy and engagement to Raheem though he couldn't believe of the loss of such a wonderful woman. "They think I killed Floyd." "did you?" "Don't tell me you feel that way too." "I don't know what to feel about you anymore." "Neither do I." Never answering the question. "I saw you that night outside my door Bernard, after I kissed him. Don't tell me you took that personal." "I'd be lying if i told you i didn't." "What do you take me for?a slut!" "I thought." "I know what you thought!" The phone was making a strange sound and she acknowledges it. "Something wrong with my phone....it keeps clicking." Bernard immediately hangs up without saying good bye. "Bernard!" she repeated. Receiving no answer as she hangs up slowly and wanting very much to tell him that she was carrying his baby. "Damn!" "What Ricky?" "He almost spilled the beans." "Did he?" "Yes he did, but he gave me enough information to go on." "Well, I got the search warrant for his mini mansion." "What about the big mansion?" The judge said he's doing his best, on the other hand we just have to wait. "What's wrong with these officials down here, are they scared of these people?" "Calm down baby, we have enough to bring him in now." "Yeah, you're right, but that confession would have been the icing on the case."

Driving at a speed of eighty five miles per hour, swaeting like a bull and high as a kite. His body's numb from the cocaine he's been sniffing all day. Trailing were two detectives in a brand new red 2000 Fire Bird Formula, respectfully ordered by superiors to be his shadow. His disappearance will cost them their jobs, and they weren't about to lose a guaranteed pension. Driving thru the roughest areas in Chicago, looking for a few great men to hold him down while taking care of all personal affairs, before leaving the country.Knowing the police would soon put the puzzles together in order to get a complete picture of what really happened. Turning up a fifth of gin as he makes a left turn on Gallen Road. Slowly riding down the toughest boulevard in town. "Hey daddy can I ride," said one of the hookers. Spotting what appeared to be a mural of Martha's late brother Danny over top of a limousine service, that's owned by Martha, Yasha, and Tiffany. Pulling up inside an old garage. "What is he doing?" asked detective Brown alertly. "I don't know but one of us better get out and mingle with the crowd in order to keep an eye on him. Anyway the garage only has one way in and out." "How you know?" "Don't worry about all that....drop me off here and circle around a few times, but don't get out." Searching his mansion thoroughly even though it had many compartments. Two hours done gone by and they haven't found anything.."Shit! I know the murder weapon is here somewhere," said ricky upsettingly. However cathy was doing great, "I got it baby!" she shouted. "That's my girl." "Guess where it was at?" "Where?" "Over top of his mantle inside the wall of the fireplace." "But....but...well, what the hell let's go capture our fugitive. "How many times you looked in that spot?" "Are we trying to be sarcastic here?" while giggling she said, "No darling, I wouldn't dare do that."

Bernard enters a elevator going underground."How did you find out us?"asked killer. "One of the sister's up the block told me about your organization." "Did she leave her name?" "No, I'm afraid not." Bernard was carrying a briefcase filled with money and traveler's checks signed already with his stamp of approval. Stepping off the elevator meticulously. "Hold up," said Killer.

Security everywhere, huge brothers walking around with full grown rottweilers, doberman pinschers, semi-automatic weapons attached to their side and head set walki-talkies with microphones. A beautiful sister approaches him wearing black Farah snug fitting jeans, a button up blouse soft grey with a v-neck that tastefully envoke feminine sensuality. "How are we today?" she whispered softly."Fine and yourself?" "Oh i'm feeling kinda freaky and kinky." Bernard didn't know what to say or do, at this time Killer comes back from somewhere."Come with me,"he said. Wrapping her right arm around Bernard's left arm, escorting him behind Killer to a remote room. Holding his briefcase firmly as he entered a large lounge area. "Have a seat,"Killer said before leaving the lounge. Resting herself upon Bernards lap, sticking her tongue down his throat. "That's enough!" Kibbles raved while snapping his finger. Immediately jumping to her feet, walking behind Kibbles, hugging his waist and kissing his neck. "What can I do for you friend?"Kibbles asked alertly."I need some good men to guard my body...the best you've got.""I'm the best I've got." "Well, what's your price?" "I'm very costly." "I know you are.""How much do you think I'm worth?" "It doesn't really matter to me, as long as you do what you get paid for." "How many days do you need of my expertise." "At this time I don't know." "Woman would you please stop! I'm trying to conduct some business here....go on somewhere!" Kibbles yelled, "Excuse the interruption.""She's beautiful." "You like her Mr.?" "Hall's the name." "Okay Mr. Hall, how does twenty thousand dollars a day sound, paid expenses?" "It's a deal." Handing him the briefcase before saying."That's seven hundred thousand dollars in cash and three hundred thousand in traveler's checks." "We don't need traveler's checks." "Trust me, you will before this is all over." "Damn! a million dollars...who's after you?" "Let's just say some very ugly friends.""Well, have no fear Kibbles is here." "Bring about twenty of your boys to my mansion in an hour, here's the address. Please, don't be late I hate late arrivals." "Oh don't worry we'll be there." Before Bernard could exit the lounge, Killer hands him a vest. "Put this on,Kibbles said,"one must protect their investment."

Resting comfortably in her custom made thong chair wearing a gold maternity muumuu. Feeling very excited about the phone conversation she'd had with Raheem. Blushing with devotion and showing complete sincerity to her wonderful engagement."What's this?" she whispered. A photo of Bernard displayed on the channel R. news. Hitting her remote to turn up the sound, wanting eagerly to hear what they were saying about her baby's father. "Wanted for the murder of Floyd Fisher." That's all she heard and it wasn't enough information missing the beginning of the reporter's statement. Flicking the channels and there was Bernard's photo being showed again. "Mr. Bernard L. Hall has been charged for the murder of Floyd Fisher two hours ago by Illinois state official, Judge Ramond f. Clerqeman. If you have any information leading to the whereabouts of the suspect, please notify authorities immediately. Do not, i repeat, do not try to apprehend the suspect yourself. He's considered to be armed and dangerous...we'll be right back after a word from our sponsors." All she could do was shake her head in a horizontal position, though deep down inside knowing he did it. Their phone conversation earlier gave him up, consequently remembering he never answered her question. "Okay you guys, we go in and get him,no horse playing...we're dealing with a cold blooded killer,with intentions to leave the state. If he comes in peace,we arrest him in peace...If not,you have the green light to take him out in pieces...Are we ready?" "Yes sir!"said the officers. Bernard preparing for battle, unfortunately he already knew they were after him. Theres no way out,all high ways,Bus stations and air ports were under heavy surveillance. Gearing up was he with out hesitation. Arriving at his front gate,were the boys and kibbles himself,with three black vans filled with artillery and men. Pressing his alarm button four times,before he answered it. "Come in fellas,"Bernard utters,as he pushed the automatic button to open the gate. Meeting them in the front of his mansion's driveway. "We're on time,"said kibbles. "Yes I see... I like that...now tell your boys to secure my whole property, and If anything comes thru that gate from here on out...kill it!" "We don't have a problem with that." "I should hope not." Doing exactly what Bernard told him to do with out interruptions. Surrounded the whole mansion,some in trees, others camouflage themselves on ground. entering Bernard's mansion spent,from all that freaking he's been doing all week,every night. Bernard stood at the top of his marble stairs watching kibbles relaxing on his sofa,he said."Your job is outside not in here, so would be so kind and leave." Out of respect kibbles remove himself. Slowly walking back to his bedroom,pausing for a minute or two,rubbing his head mesmerized. walking towards his dresser,staring in the mirror chapfallenly,and pulling out a glod tray filled with cocaine. Sniffing a large amount before guzzling a whole fifth of gin. sniffing repeatedly while throwing his head back from the rush he received though his heart's beating rapidly, Arriving infront of his premises with badges out, and to their surprise the gate was opened. What they didn't know was that the front entrance was left opened for a reason, Having know idea of the fate before them,however they were fully equiped and ready for battle. Entering alertly and leading the troops were Detectives Ricky and Cathy. "I have this strange feeling,"said Cathy,"he knows we are here." A woman's intuition is something most men ignore however,we need to take heed to it. Ricky wasn't trying to hear a thing,his mind's set on one thing and one thing only, that's capturing Bernard. All of a sudden gun fire coming at them rapidly from all angles. "Duck down!!!...head for cover!" Ricky shouted repeatedly. Cathy laid stretch out in the grass, Ricky immediately runs to her aid. "Cover me!!!!..."he yelled. Cathy staring at the sky with her eyes and mouth wide open. "Cath...Cath...Don't die on me." "My legs are numb,"she cried sadly. "Don't worry the ambulance are on the way." Placing her head upon his lap while rubbing her hands gently. She started coughing,he wipes her mouth,and in a strainful way she said. "I have something very important to tell you." "Save your breath honey because your gonna need it." "I'm pregnant." "You're what?!" "You heard me?.." " And you jeopardized our baby?" "Yes i did,to watch your ass, ain't no sense...Raising a baby alone." "I'm sorry sweetheart." "I know you are." "Sir the helicopter is here,"said officer Gray. "Is the S.W.A.T. TEAM and national guards on the way?" "Yes sir." The helicopter landed. "What the hell happened here?" "Commander sir we have a warren't for this man's arrest,for the murder of Floyd Fisher." "So why didn't you arrest him,..and how come ten officers are wounded plus that beautiful young lady,who just aboared the helicopter?" "Commander Sir,he refuses to cooperate,and he's not alone." "Oh is that so...I'll show him who's boss around here.""Commander Sir the phone." "Thank you soldier." At this time the commander's having a deep conversation with the two star General,though Detective Ricky's becoming very impatient and blood boiling for revenge, he had to maintain. "okay you guys, impermissible is not in my vocabulary today,we will do what ever we have to do to get him out of there." Ricky's so glad to hear those words coming from the Commander's mouth. The mansio's now surround with police officers,specail crim units and arm forces. "What is this guys name?"asked the commander. "Bernard L.Hall." "I suppose the L stands for LUNATIC!!!.." "I don't know Sir." "That wasn't a question,pass me the microphone. Mr. Bernard L Hall this is Commander Simmone...We have a warrent for your arrest,so I suggest you come out with your hands up high,..Quietly before more people gets hurt...Inculding yourself." Waiting patiently,however, there was no response. Kibbles boys were not giving up, plus it was to late. the Commander tells the first rank of officers to go in,and thats exactly what they do. Guns ringing, bullets singing and smoke filled the air, simultaneously officers were dropping. "Send in the next rank,"said the commander. Two helicopters hovered the area with four sharp shooter, nailing Kibbles boys to the trees, grass and cement which lead to Bernard's driveway. Killer shoots a missile, destroying one of the helicopters and the other disappears. This was a Vietnam War resurrected, blood, body parts and debris everywhere. Kibbles throws two grenades killing six officers who were creeping from his rear and after the smoke cleared he said"Stupid ass mutha'fucka's..what you thought I was new at this!....Ha! You better ask somebody bitch ass pigs.....Killer! "YO!" "You alright?" "Do bitches got tit?" "That nigg Bernard set us up." "You right about that." "We'll take care of him later, let's get the fuck outta here!" What they don't know won't hurt, and no one's escaping. Martha sorely watching the news and wanting seriously to help Bernard, hence being stunned at the performance he displayed left her speechless. The commander on the other hand couldn't take no more of his bullshit."He wanna play hard ball, drop men on the roof, now!" Listen young man this is your last warning come out with your hands up!" said the commander viciously. "Commander sir the phone." "Yes." things were heating up. Explosion after explosion. "Shit!" "What's the problem commander?" Ricky asked. "I'll tell you what the problem is....they want this fucker alive. I can't believe it after all the trouble he's put us thru." Ricky totally ignored that, he's going to kill Bernard the first chance he gets for his future wife. Not to mention she's pregnant and going thru complications unfortunately the baby might not live and he's aware of that."Commander, this scum bag cannot live!" Ricky raved. "Son, it's no longer my choice,the Governor's calling for a state of emergency......but you're not an officer in this state and things do happen,get my drift?"Ricky immediately comprehended with a smirk he said "Yes sir." "Becareful...listen up men i need ten to go with my officer Ricky." Slowly but surely Kibbles boys were being captured and destroyed. "Killer you see what I see?" asked Kibbles. "Yes, we have to make a move man or our ass is history like the rest of them." "Listen you two, you are surrounded, do the smart thing and give up," said Captain Reed. "Yo man, I ain't goin out like that....see you in heaven or hell baby."said killer. "Like wise." In slow motion they stood, yelling and spraying their semi automatic weapons hitting seven officials. "Duck down!" yelled the sergent. A helicopter hovers out of nowhere shooting Killer sixteen times with an A.K. forty seven, ripping ligaments to pieces. Seeing his best friend destroyed right before his eyes terrified his heart. Jumping to his feet yelling"AAAAAHHHHHHHHH!" releasing shells, however his end was near. One shot entered his forehead the size of a quarter, exiting the size of a tennis ball and blowing his head right off his shoulders. Bernard's all alone now, standing in the livingroom of his mansion sipping and sniffing, carrying a double barrell sixteen eagle pump shot gun. Drilling a hole in his ceiling right above him, acknowledging it fearlessly. He pumps the shot gun and fires four times towards the sound of the drilling, hitting two officers. One of them falls thru the ceiling landing on his head, while the other slipped, hanging himself from his own hang rope. Bernard shoots thru the hole in the ceiling several times. "How dare you fuck with me!" he said drunkenly. "This is officer Ricky, Bernard, do yourself a favor." "And what's that?" "Turn yourself in." "Can I ask you a question...officer Ricky?" "Go right ahead." "Hows....ah....the little bitch doing?" "Who are you talking about?" "You know...know...who I'm talking about." "No I don't, refresh my memory." "Ya' partner, the beautiful little bitch....who wanted to give me some of that pussy, but you cock blocked me." "Alright, you asked for it!" "Officer Ricky is a cockblocker,cockblocker,cockblocker, a fuckin cockblocker!" "Let down the tear gas," Ricky shouted. "OH SHITTT!" Bernard shouts, running towards the basement of his mansion firing at the ceiling with every stride, tearing plaster. "Excuse me commander sir." "What is it private?" "Ricky's on the line." "Yes Ricky." Letting the commander know that they were inside. "Good job," the commander said, "Don't do anything until me and the psychiatrist arrives....by the way that partner of yours is doing perfectly alright, she'll be walking soon." His face lit up, hence being excited to do anything to Bernard especially kill him. Martha was so nervous, at the edge of her seat as she stared at the t.v. contemplating. "Mr.Bernard, my name is Mr. webster Andrews. I'm your doctor." "What kinda' doctor mutha'fucka'?" Bernard barricaded himself in the cellar of his mansion. "A psychiatrist." "So you come to tell me, I'm crazy...I know..i know.....I killed everybody, but I'm not crazy. Your the ones who's crazy....I'm just a psycho, you stupid motha'fucka's....HHHAAAAAA!" "Commander sir." "Yes private." "There's a woman on line two, i have know idea how she got thru but she said she's his baby's mother." "That fucker has a baby?" "Excuse me commander sir, she's expecting." "Give me that phone private." At this time the commander speaks with Martha and the doctor continued with his conversation though Bernard wasn't paying any attention.

Martha immediately slipped on some garments and her nanny asked. "Wher are you going sister Bari?" "Down to Mr. Hall's mansion to talk some sense in him." "I have orders to look after you carefully." "Well, you're not breaking your orders...get dressed and let's go." "Are we taking the limo?" "Yes we are." Wasting no time she storms out the door, and the nanny calls for security to follow them. Bernard became very hostile, firing his gun at nothing. "I have something to tell you," said the commader to the shrink. "Let's hear it." whispering in his ear,"That's just the remedy we need," said the doctor. "You think it'll work?" "Well commader, I don't know, it's only one way to find out." Bernard was on every news and radio station in town. One hour later, calling to the front gate of the mansion letting the officers know of Martha's arrival. Twany and Barbara were praying for Bernard's capture in spite of all the trouble he's put them thru everyone wishes him life, not death, the whole state. The newsrooms and radio stations took a pole, ninety five percent of the population wanna see him live nevertheless five percent wants him dead. Martha enters the mansion eagerly concerned for she knew he needed to know the truth and being cock sure, that's what she had to tell him,hoping it will make him turn himself in. Like everybody else Martha would be in for a big surprise. The commader greeted her and said"Are you ready?" "I didn't come all this way for nothing." "Give it a shot." Bernard became very quiet,he went from a wild beast to an angel. "Bernard....Bernard....I love you dearly." "Martha is that you?" "Yes it's me baby." Everyone started smiling including doc, all thinking to themselves, it's finally over,four hours of destruction."Martha, what are you doing here?" "I came to help you baby, and tell you some great news...that is, if you wanna hear it." Tears dropped from his eyes, though loving this woman more than anything on this planet. He did all of this just to see if she would come to his aid. His heart's finally satisfied however prison wasn't in his plans. He knew he had to strike up a conversation to make her angry so she would leave and he can take care of business. Knowing his soul's to corrupt to live on, atleast that what he thought. Silence rose and no one knew what to say however the doc tells her to speak on. "Bernard are you okay in there?" she asked with tears rolling down her cheeks. "No, I'm not okay...why did you do the things you did to me?" "I'm sorry baby, I was being selfish." "Why did you fuck the town?" "What?!" "You heard me." Wanting badly to spaz on him for what he just said,however letting it slide and the doc shakes his head no. He seen her body language and immediately directed her attention somewhere else. "I was trying to make you jealous baby and i was wrong," she said. "You damn right you was wrong you filthy slut." "Oh, hell no, he didn't!" she whispered to herself. He predicted what she said, and said. "Yes i did!" "If you must know Bernard, I"m pregnant!" "Oh, don't tell me ...were you freddy's mother in the movie nightmare on elm street?" "Why are you talking to me like this?" "Woman you ruined my life, and know you decide to prance up here letting me know you're pregnant." "Will you hear me out first?" "No you listen!You get married to the rich ass ghetto man and get pregnant. Then you lie and tell me I was your first, but he was fuckin you the night before I proposed to your trifling ass." Cutting him off. "Wait a Goddamn minute , this is yo' baby I'm carrying, not his,... okay!" feeling lightheaded, trembling, getting highly upset behind all of the terrible things he's said to her.Bernard laughed and said. "So you're saying it's my dick that did that?" He really didn't believe she was pregnant by him. He truly thought they were using her to get to him and taking part in their whole scheme. "Good try," he said "Now bitch get the fuck outta' here!....The sound of your voice makes me sick!" She tried holding it in, in spite of all the cruel things he said to her, wiping her eyes before saying"You ain't shit! Bernard L. Hall and I hate that I ever met you...don't worry about this baby she'll be well taken care of even if her sorry ass daddy neglected her. You'll come around soon, when the judge give yo' ass all that time. Don't call me, talking about where's my baby....just remember you don't have one, that ain't what I said, that's what you said." "BITCH PLEASE!!!!" "FUCK YOU BERNARD!" she cried strutting out the basement of his mansion. "You already did!" he screamed repeatedly. "What's next smart doc?"asked the commander sarcastically. The only way they could get into the basements cellar was to blow the door open, and who knows what type of artillery he had down there. As Martha slowly opens the front door to Bernard's mansion, she heard a loud boom sound and dropped to the floor. Bernard had unlocked the cellar door before blowing his own head completely off. That's not all, four female bodies were found in trunks decomposed and decapitated.

Five months after Bernard's suicide,Martha and Raheem had their million dollar wedding in Africa as planned.Martha gave birth to a beautiful 8lb. 7oz. little girl named Halima....she looked just like her father.

THE END...

EPILOGUE

Powerless to powerful, thoughts of jealousy entering the hearts of the Beholders. Secrets, passions,jaunty life styles and ironic love affairs.. Invidious minds, with in the circles of their environment and no one noticed. A destructive force of energy was being born, like whiskey in a bottle, It can do no harm until someone uses it. Martha, Yasha and Tiffany Ghetto Princesses wanting the best that life can offer and will go to the highest extremes to receive it. Power,money,respect, and equal opportunities, the strongest elements in the corporate world...Men watch out, cause here they come, sisters with attitudes.

DEDICATIONS

MY WIFE CRYSTAL JEFFRIES,MY CHIDREN AND GRANDCHILDREN.

MY MOTHER LINDA MARRIE JEFFRIES, R.I.P.

AFRICAQUE "MESHA" SMITH FUTRELL,R.I.P.

SHAWN CORNELL McBRIDE,R.I.P.

MELODY McKENZIE,R.I.P.

EDGAR SCOTT "TWIN" BROWN,R.I.P.

BILLY JORDAN,R.I.P.

FARRAGUT HOUSES BROOKLNY,N.Y. 4BUILDING..13FLOOR.

THE AUTHOR.... XAVIER JEFFRIES...

MORE BOOKS TO COME..TITLED..

DEEPER THAN THE GRAVE.

AWAKENING TO MISERY.

SISTERS FOR LIFE.

CLOSE DA' CASKET.

ROAD RAGE.

JINNS.

CPSIA information can be obtained at www.ICGtesting.com
Printed in the USA
LVOW10s2251020314

375778LV00011B/168/P